I0160522

THE GENERAL BOOK OF THE TAROT

THE GENERAL BOOK OF THE TAROT

A.E. Thierens, Ph.D.

WILDSIDE PRESS

Published by
Wildside Press, LLC
P.O. Box 301
Holicong, PA 18928-0301 USA
www.wildsidepress.com

Wildside Press Edition: MMIII

CONTENTS

CONTENTS

INTRODUCTION

IF ever a book should be written on the Romance of Symbolism, its hypothesis of interpretation, its traditional and imputed histories, a considerable space would be allotted assuredly to Tarot-cards; while seeing that at this day there is more concern in the subject than was felt even in the past, there would be a call not only to survey that which lies behind us, a strange field of speculation and reverie, but the prospect extending in front, since every year brings forth some new proposition and provides material for future imaginative flights. It is very curious to contrast those comparatively sober terms in which Court de Gebelin introduced his discovery of the cards,* though he sought to prove that their origin was in Ancient Egypt, with the fantastic declamations of Éliphas Lévi, who affirmed not only that they were the Alphabet of Enoch, Hermes Trismegistus and Cadmus but the Gospel of all Gospels, a synthesis of science and the universal key of the Kabbalah.

De Gebelin was a man of learning at his own period and remained within the circle of facts, actual or supposed, as he saw and read them. His successor was a man of extravagant mind, who contemplated past and future alike through a glass of vision, and so beheld all faërie unfold its images. The occult happenings of the past became in the process as much a matter of invention as his own notions. The inventions were decorative and were even characterised at times by a magian quality of intuition; but in most cases his record of past events was like his reading of things to come. His tale of the Knights Templar, his intimations on the Rosy Cross, his survey of alchemical literature are in much the same category as his prognostications about a parliament of nations under an universal monarchy ruled by a King of France. He

* *Monde Primitif, analysé et comparé avec le Monde Moderne*, par M. Court de Gebelin, 9 vols. The account and examination of the Tarot will be found in Vol. VIII, published in 1781.

discovered the religion behind all religions, a fountain-source from which they issued in their day and into which all return. This was the Secret Tradition of Israel ; but it proves to be a Tradition of his own making, which falsifies all the literature, and he had not read the texts from which he claimed to draw. He had glanced there and here at a few records of the subject and distorted them in the magic crystal of his seership. He took up the Tarot, and just as a cartomancist shuffles and deals and lays out its picture-symbols for the reading of things to come, so did he divine their past. He adopted the speculations of De Gebelin, and they dilated in his own mind. He dressed up the Trumps Major in Egyptian vestures and affirmed that he had restored the Tarot in its primitive hieroglyphical form. By a fortunate chance there had preceded him in 1857 another fantasiast, J. F. Vaillant, with a gift in etymologies, more stupefying than anything produced before him.* Between them there deployed all Babylon and all its idols. But Egypt loomed behind Babylon and the Kabbalah behind Egypt. It is post-Talmudic in unadorned fact, but for them it was older than Moses and older even than Abraham. In fine, behind the Kabbalah there was, and remains among us, the Book of Thoth, and this was the Tarot, within which was the light unlimited of its endless range of meanings that had never passed into writing but dwelt implicitly in both, above all in Lévi's mind. And a day came when he made his great discovery which had never entered previously into the heart of scholiast or commentator. The Tree of Life in Kabbalism has 22 Paths by which the Sephiroth or Numerations are connected one with another and late Kabbalism had married these Paths to the 22 Letters of the Hebrew Alphabet. But the Tarot Trumps Major are also 22, and Éliphas Lévi proclaimed another marriage, constituting a Trinity in unity of Cards and Paths and Letters. It has been the joy of all Occult hierophants and their believing disciples through the decades that followed. On all these Lévi has exercised a great influence in French circles, and seeing that Tarot expository literature is French almost exclusively, he calls for consideration at length when estimating expository values.

* *Les Romes* appeared at the date in question and maintained that the history of the Tarot is lost in the night of time, but everything justifies the hypothesis that it is of Indo-Tartarian origin and that it has been transmitted to modern times by the Romany tribes of his title.

It was not in the least needful but was pleasant, if opportunity offered, to find that there were others before him who knew and had used to some purpose the Tarot keys. As a fact, there was St. John on Patmos, the proof being that he wrote his Book of Revelations in 22 chapters. The Apocalypse henceforward, for true initiates, became an exposition of Tarot Trumps. It had not occurred to Lévi or to those who followed him that the arrangement of scripture texts in divisions called chapters is unhappily a late device. There was also Louis Claude de Saint-Martin, who was one of *les vrais initiés*, and he had written a certain *Tableau*, setting forth the relations between God, Man and the Universe. He broke it up into numbered parts which reached the same total, so the *Tableau Naturel* arises out of the Tarot and returns therein. After what manner the cards and the sections belong to one another in either case, it was not to be expected perhaps that a French Magus should unfold, though he held the key of all things, so the allocation remains a mystery even to this day, while the Lévi successors in France reproduce their master's dogmas from generation to generation.

Hereof is the Tarot in its literary history, from the pre-French Revolution *Monde Primitif* of Court de Gebelin to the year 1870, when it occurred to P. Christian (Paul Pitois), *ancien bibliothecaire* that the History of Magic might be extended further, with profit, by the gentle art of invention. The Franco-Prussian war stood on the threshold of events, Éliphas Lévi had been silent for five years and was forgotten for the time being, though still in print. It was safe to borrow something of his motives and manner, as also from the spectacular findings in his glass of vision ; so Christian borrowed accordingly, and his tale of *La Fatalité à travers les temps et les peuples* is the *Histoire de la Magie* of Lévi, retold after another manner and with more liberal and frequent appeal to the repertory of the Father of Lies. Christian had none of those literary gifts which adorn the pages of Lévi, but his inventions are highly sensational and often microscopical in detail. It seems probable even that, like his predecessor, he began by convincing himself (a) that things should have happened in that or in this way and therefore did, (b) that his divinatory devices foretold the future, at least now and then. It is precisely this kind of mischief which begets itself in others, and altogether I am not surprised that Christian's *L'Homme Rouge des Tuileries*, which followed—I think—his

Histoire de la Magie, has become of authority among Grimoires and is sought eagerly, or that he is still quoted off and on for his Tarot views.

A space of fifteen years elapsed, and *circa* 1885 a group of neo-Martinists began to be formed in Paris, with Papus— Dr. Gérard Encausse—at their head. As it happened that notwithstanding the two-and-twenty sections of his *Tableau Naturel,* Saint-Martin contributed nothing to Tarot lore, had in all probability never glanced at the mysterious card-symbols, and abandoned early and definitely all occult workings, the Martinism of the late XIXth century signified, as a name only, that its followers had their eyes turned to the esoteric tradition of the West, rather than that of the East, and in their preoccupation were thinly Christian rather than theosophical in the sense of Modern Theosophy, through which some of them had passed and had come forth unsatisfied. The Master in Chief of Papus was always Éliphas Lévi, to whom his occult notions are referable in the last resource, whose Kabbalism is his Kabbalism and whose Tarot is his Tarot. Papus worked indefatigably at these subjects and extended them on every side, producing great inventions, with a certain laborious sincerity, as I shall be disposed always to think. But, like those who preceded and those who have come after him, Papus was an occultist, not a mystic, and from my point of view the pictorial symbols of *les imagiers du moyen âge,* as Oswald Wirth terms them, unfold their meanings in this other and higher light.

The Martinist School, its connections and derivatives, produced their Tarots, *sub nomine* Falconnier, *sub nomine* Alta, *sub nomine* Oswald Wirth, and there were yet other artists and diviners, some borrowing lights from one another and some kindling an occasional torch or a casual flash on their own part. The Monographs multiplied, and the Marquis Stanislas de Guiata produced a sequence of treatises wherein all occultism unfolded from the Trumps Major. There was no end to the activities, with the Lévi pageants always in the background and in the forefront often.

When twenty-five years had elasped in this manner and the Tarot Bibliography had attained considerable dimensions, the War of 1914 engulfed all the Schools and all their brave imaginings ; and when it was in fine suspended by the figurative peace of Versailles, the Schools emerged but slowly from the weltering chaos and were shorn of their chief personalities, their adornments and appeal. The names of some of them are with us at this day, centered in a little group at Lyons. But French occultism, apart from specific schools and incorporated pretensions, seems very much alive, and Oswald Wirth produced recently the most decorative Tarot study, so far as form is concerned, which has appeared since we first heard of the subject.* His attention is directed to the Trumps Major solely and he has little to say on the divinatory side of of the subject, that so-called practical side which engrosses most persons who would call themselves Tarot students. It is none of my own business, but it is clear from my knowledge of the literature that under this aspect there is room for new treatment. Dr. Thierens has approached it from an astrological standpoint in the work which these preliminary pages are designed to introduce. I have been led to do so because very little has been printed previously on the zodiacal attributions of the cards and because it happens that I am acquainted with unpublished divinatory methods making use of these attributions for many years past in one of the occult circles.† There is a literature of the Tarot which has not emerged so far into the light of day and some of it is excessively curious. It was said of old in a very different connexion: *Quod tenet nunc teneat donec de medio fiat ;* and I do not know whether certain subsisting difficulties will be taken ultimately out of the way, so that the theoretical and practical speculations of such circles may be compared with those brought forward in public ways during recent and earlier years. In this manner we should have at least the subject general of the Tarot expanded fully.

Meanwhile Dr. Thierens has approximated more than anyone else towards a valid interpretation of Tarot Trump Major No. XII, being the Hanged Man. From Court de Gebelin to Papus and Stanislas de Guaita, not excluding Oswald

* *Le Tarot des Imagiers du Moyen Âge*, 1927, accompanied by a separative portfolio of coloured plates and with many illustrations in the text.

† Oswald Wirth has a short excursus on Astrology at the end of his work, in which he enumerates the zodiacal implicities allocated to the four elements, but no Tarot connection is suggested. It is rather curious that a study of the *Sepher Zetzirah* in conjunction with the Tree of Life and the triple marriage effected by Éliphas Lévi has not produced speculations long since on the astronomical and astrological correspondences of the Tarot Trumps.

Wirth himself, all published exoteric meanings are utterly remote from the true significance of this most pregnant symbol. In my *Pictorial Key to the Tarot* and in the Little Key which accompanies Miss Pamela Colman Smith's complete set of the cards, produced long ago under my own auspices, there was said concerning it that which was possible at the time. I will give now one further indication. The human figure of the symbol is suspended head downward and as such it is comparable to the Microprosopus or God of Reflections in the so-called Great Symbol or Double Triangle of Solomon, prefixed by Lévi to this *Dogme et Rituel de la Haute Magie*, being the frontispiece of the first volume.* It follows that the true symbol belonging to Trump Major No. XII, though it is by no means that of Lévi, is not a Hanged Man at all ; but it will continue to be depicted in this manner unless and until the Greater Arcana are issued by the authority of another Secret Circle, which so far has never testified officially concerning itself in the outer channels of research.

I have said that every year brings forth some new consideration, and Dr. Thierens promises another work, while the speculation which has just been adventured speaks of things unattempted and yet conceived in the mind. There is no intention signified ; but I know what emblems would adorn it. How things will stand with the Tarot in days to come may loom therefore vaguely ; but obviously there are activities to come. There is, however, one side of the subject on which no horizon opens. As to where the Trumps Major originated, how and with whom, there is no conclave of adepts to tell us and no isolated student, holding evidential warrants. At the moment we can look only for more speculations and more dreams to come.

ARTHUR EDWARD WAITE.

---

* See my annotated translation, entitled *Transcendental Magic : Its Doctrine and Ritual*, new and revised edition, 1923.

THE GENERAL
BOOK OF THE TAROT

I

THE DOCTRINE

THE knowledge of the Tarot, handed down to us through the ages, and as we find it at the beginning of the XXth century, can be traced in the writings of many authors. Its most perfect interpretations until now are to be found in the works of Eliphas Lévi (*Dogme et Rituel de la Haute Magie*) and Dr. Papus (*Le Tarot des Bohémiens* and *Le Tarot Divinatoire*). These may be said to represent the best results of earlier times, including Eteilla and P. Christian.

A booklet by S. L. MacGregor Mathers, an author well known for his works on subjects relating to the Kabbalah, quotes J. F. Vaillant (1857) as saying " that it (the Tarot) belongs to the beginning of our time, to the epoch of the preparation of the zodiac . . ." and ". . . The great divinity *Ashtarot, As-Tarot,* is no other than the Indo-Tartar *Tan-tara,* the *Tarot,* the Zodiac."

This is curious, and we wonder if one or the other ever worked out so much as a real scheme of this relationship between the Tarot system and the zodiacal principles. If so, as far as we know, it did not appear publicly.

Another well-known author on ancient mysteries and symbolism, Arthur Edward Waite, who revised and introduced an English edition of Papus' *Tarot of the Bohemians*, by A. P. Morton, has presented us with a still more precious booklet entitled *The Key to the Tarot*, from which we quote :

" The Tarot is symbolism ; it speaks no other language and offers no other signs."

And we would add that true symbolism is always the figurative rendering of cosmological truth or natural principles and laws in visual linguistic or mental image. If astrological symbolism does the same, why should we not seek for a correlation between the two systems ? And if further we come to the conclusion, as we must, that both systems give a rendering of the process of creation itself, totally and definitely, then the two must practically present the same point of view, and a comparison between them must not only be instructive but may elucidate both.

In the present work, it is our ardent desire to join with Mr. Waite, " so that the effect of current charlatanism and unintelligence may be reduced to a minimum."

We shall abstain from any special criticism and pass over the more ancient literature on the subject—by such writers as Eteilla, Court de Gebelin, P. Christian, etc.—literature which has been mostly embodied in the works mentioned above, which we specially recommend to those readers who wish to study the subject exhaustively. The best Tarot cards are those drawn by Miss Pamela Colman Smith, published in England, and issued with Mr. Waite's booklet. The designs on these cards appear to be the most pure in their symbolical details, and to be drawn with inspiration and clear vision, though in general the ancient description or traditional rendering has evidently been followed.

The symbolical system of the Tarot consists of 78 picture cards of which 22 constitute the *Major Arcana* or *Trumps Major*, 56 (4 × 14) the *Minor Arcana, Trumps Minor.* As far as we know the idea of analogy with the zodiacal mysteries has, until now, found no further practical realisation than a rather diffuse comparison of the four ' colours ' or suits in the Lesser Arcana with the Four Elements in the Cosmos, as we find them in astrology.

THE LESSER ARCANA

The pack of cards of the Lesser Arcana has been generally acknowledged as the origin of our ordinary playing-cards, though subsequent authorities do not wholly agree upon this point. Thus we find Dr. Papus saying :

". . . wands have become the clubs (or trèfles) of our present playing-cards, cups have become hearts, swords have become spades and pentacles have become diamonds." (Chapter I.)

Mr. Waite in his *Key* says :

". . . wands or sceptres . . . diamonds . . . cups correspond to hearts . . . swords answer to clubs . . ."

and finally pentacles " which are the prototype of spades." (P. 37.)

In MacGregor Mathers' booklet we find *in extenso* the following table :

Italian	*French*	*English*	*Answering to*
Bastoni	Bâtons	Wands, Sceptres or Clubs	Diamonds
Coppé	Coupes	Cups, Chalices or Goblets	Hearts
Spadé	Epées	Swords	Spades
Denari	Deniers	Money, Circles or Pentacles	Clubs

The discrepancies are evident. Furthermore questions may arise as to how one writer could call swords, clubs, while linguistically a wand and a club originally mean the same thing, and cover the same meaning, *viz.* that of a detached part of a living tree ; and how is it that another could see wands answering to diamonds and a third make pentacles clubs ? Evidently a sword must be a ' spade ' and a wand must be a ' club,' the names being virtually identical. There seems, however, some difficulty regarding the other two. I object to the usage as given by Papus and MacGregor Mathers and can easily bring forward proof against it. Important differences like these, found in the writings of the principal authors on the subject, show that something is wanting in the understanding of the doctrine itself and the ' why ' has been lost, or at least partially. The quest for this doctrine must be fully worth the trouble—and we shall endeavour, in the following pages, to follow it up to its origin in general cosmological principles.

Now the first thing we wish to point out is this : the system of the Tarot is so important, that no explanation can be accepted as satisfactory other than that which acknowledges it as a general outline of Creation itself, which ever was, and ever continues, pervading every creature and everything with its principles as a divine immanence.

Therefore Papus is quite right in stating, that " each card of the Tarot represents a symbol, a number and an idea."

At the basis of Creation are the Four Cosmic Elements, as they were symbolically mentioned by visionaries such as Ezechiel and St. John of Patmos, and taught by astrology of old. It requires no extraordinary intuition of the occult student to recognise in the four colours of our playing-cards or the four suits of the Tarot's Lesser Arcana those four basic Elements : Fire, Earth, Air and Water. The question remains however : Which is which ?

There must have been a time when knowledge about these matters was nearer at hand than is the case nowadays ; the symbols speak for it. A student of Occultism has to pay attention to symbols above all. So what do they tell us ?

WANDS.—As a matter of fact, curiously enough, all authors agree in naming wands or clubs in the first place. In our set of playing cards the figurative symbol for it is the trefoil (French *trèfle*)—*tri-folio*—and Mr. Ouspensky draws the wands bearing leaves which in many instances appear to be threefold—at least they should be. The trefoil or shamrock has always been considered a luck-charm, *porte-bonheur*.*

* In a very special way the four-bladed shamrock is considered to convey luck. This evidently means that the luck will be effective or real, practical, when " the Three fall into the Four " according to the old saying in the Stanza's of Dzyan.

B

It is built upon the scheme of the triangle, symbol of Trinity, and the totality of the figure appears also in the masonic ' trefoil,' which is an emblem of the Divine Trinity together with the principle of activity, indicated by the staff or wand itself, eventually crossed as in the ancient emblem.

In a way we must regard this symbol as revealing the highest conception of Creation : Trinity pure and simple with only the rudiment of activity indicated, standing still above the circle, as far or as soon as the latter suggests Motion. So wands, clubs or trèfles are most certainly meant as the symbol of the highest element in Creation.

The question has often been put as to whether, in the astrological idea of creation, Air or Fire ought to be regarded as the highest element. The answer depends upon the standpoint we take. In the highest cosmological or cosmo-philosophical sense it is Fire ; in a cosmo-practical or cosmo-natural sense it is Air, as *the Secret Doctrine* undoubtedly makes us understand, where the dissolution of cosmos at the end of a Manvantara is treated of and it is said that the Earth is dissolved or engulfed by the Waters, Water evaporated by Fire, and finally Fire disappearing in the Air. Here Air is acting as the atmosphere of the globe or system disappearing. So for all practical uses, in astrology as well, it is Air which is able to give the highest expression of the Divine. As the atmosphere of a globe it is the link between it and the Ether of space, carrying the rays of the divine solar centre as well as those of the relatively ' demoniacal ' surroundings to the other elements, constituting the existence of the globe. In a similar way the suit of wands will appear to be something of a link between the Lesser and the Greater Arcana. This will be dealt with later.

Taken in this way Air is ' the bearer of the Message ' from the Divine (Ether) or Unmanifest to the terrestrial or manifested worlds. And wands are the significators of the messages in detail and of intelligences, which astrologically correspond to Air, consequently of higher thought and mental processes.

The magic wand is used to convey the divine or at least semi-divine will-power of the Self acting as a magician into the world of phenomena.

As in Macrocosm the Message goes out to the Water (the emotional element of experience in the Soul), and Metals (sensatory elements of understanding in the Body), so in microcosm, on Earth, a wand may be used to find out water and metals in the soil. This may seem curious, but is pure analogy.

From days of old a wand or staff was used to ' chastise,' i.e. to render chaste or pure, the undisciplined or disobedient, a penalty as much symbolical as corporeal, the staff being at the same time the insignum of a superior will-power or supervision.

Hermes-Mercury, Lord of the Element of Air, of Knowledge and Understanding, Bearer of the Message of the Gods, carried as his emblem, his well-known Wand encompassed by two snakes and bearing a cup on top. He was called Trismegistus, the ' threefold ' Great (or the Great Trefoil ₹), which might also be translated as Lord or Magister of the register of Trefoil, King of the Wands.

And the pilgrim, who went to hear the word of deliverance and to gather knowledge, took up a staff, not only as a walking-stick but also as a symbol of his quest. The latter finds illustration in the legend of Tannhauser, whose ‘ sin ’ (ignorance) was so great, that its expiation could be expected as little as the budding of new leaves on his (dead) pilgrim’s staff, the latter being evidently taken as an image of the principle of the ‘ wand ’ in his own soul. And when, by the force of Love, a higher understanding budded forth in himself, this fact was symbolised by the apparition of a fresh green leaf on his staff.

The ancient Norsemen, highly susceptible to symbolism, wrote their signs of communication or messages on *stafe*, wands, which became the origin of the later word *Buchstabe* in German.

PENTACLES.—Generally cups are named in the second place but are at the same time identified with hearts. We agree that the hearts come in the second place of the hierarchy of the Tarot suits, but do not see, that they should be ‘ cups.’ Of course we understand that the heart has been said to be the ‘ cup ’ receiving and containing the divine life, etc. But still we disagree and even think the parable rather superficial, for it leaves the mutual relation of the three remaining elements in a distorted condition. Moreover the symbolical names, as given by the different authors mentioned, do not agree.

If, taken as a whole, wands stand for the Message of the Macrocosm or Ideation, as Air transfers the message from the Ether, and if we take for granted, that the imagination of the Tarot system was meant and given for cosmo-practical or cosmo-natural usage, then we must be prepared to find in the remaining three suits the elements of (say : ' human ') spirit, soul and body incarnate (i.e. as they appear in the manifested world), thus constituting together the microcosm *in toto*. Astrology gives for the three the symbols : Sun, Moon and Ascendant (Earth). We should rather say : the Fifth, the Ninth and the First house in the horoscopic circle. Compare our second volume on Cosmology, entitled *Elements of Astrology*.

If now, to indicate these three principles, we dispose of a pentacle, a cup and a sword, it is most surely the pentacle on the coin of gold or within the circle, which relates to the heart and the principle of spirit, located in the Fifth house. For here the human spirit with its *fivefold* nature originates and here the fivefold magic or creative force resides. It is difficult to see what other meaning the pentacle could have than the symbolising of the Fifth house in Creation, which is the heart to every living being. There is not the least shade of doubt that in the horoscope the beginning of the spiritual spiral lies in the Fifth house. Gold is the metal ruled by the Sun, lord of the Fifth sign, Leo, the heart of the solar system. So pentacles or golden coins are the hearts in playing-cards and correspond to the element Fire.

The symbol in playing-cards is drawn in the natural likeness of a heart. There is as little doubt concerning the element Fire, because, as every astrologer knows and realises, spirit, soul and body stand in the same relation as Fire, Water and Earth. Compare the *Secret Doctrine*, where ' a centre of Fire and Water ' is the origin for a new incarnation on Earth. Curiously enough, divination never has interpreted ' hearts ' in any other way than as symbolising things belonging to the heart or coming forth from it. In so far this ' colour ' has been well understood. But its gold is a spiritual symbol and has as yet nothing to do with ' money.' It is in the soul and not in the spirit, that the idea of repayment is forged, though no doubt the spiritual gold may be said to be the origin of all that will later on appear as vulgar money.

CUPS.—The soul is ruled by the Moon and the element Water, as is well known in astrology. It is in the cosmic principle of Soul, or in other words : in the Cosmic Soul, that the truth of the philosophic statement, *Panta Rei* (everything in the world is flowing), is revealed. And there is no better symbol for the specific nature of the soul *in concreto* than that of a cup or chalice, which contains the Liquor of Life. The cup is really suggestive enough with regard to the element Water.

When Jesus prayed : " Lord let this chalice pass from me," He indicated something which He feared would fill his *soul* with bitterness. And in the Last Supper He passed along the chalice of brotherhood amongst the disciples, as a sign of *soul*-union, a custom still followed by the churches of Christianity and in days of old by King Arthur at the meetings of the Round Table. The Christian churches lay much stress on the mystic happenings with the Holy

Chalice on the altar, the receiver of Divine Light and Blessings. Herein we may see a demonstration of the mystery of Christ, Son of the Heart (that is, the Sun in the Solar system), *Divine Soul* (the ' Father ' being Divine Spirit) using the persona of Jesus as Its Cup or vessel (*vahana*).

In one of the masonic High Grades the cup reappears with the symbolic ' supper ' of brotherhood.

The quest of the Holy Graal—the legendary Holy Chalice or Cup of Felicity—shadowed forth in the ritual of the church—is well known to represent the thirst or solicitude of the *soul* for the spiritual water or wine of Life Divine. The Graal itself symbolises the shape of a human or superhuman personality, a soul of human nature, filled or ' fulfilled ' by this Divine Essence, by which it becomes a Holy One, a Master or Elder Brother. So it means the quest of the common human soul for the Master Soul.

Cups or beakers are used throughout the world to drink ' welcome ' and friendship, i.e. to express the idea of soul-union : something like " my soul drinks from the same liquor as yours," viz. the liquor of life or of renovation of life ; " my soul meets yours in the drinking of the wine divine, and so knows that we are brothers."

Among playing-cards cups cannot be anything else but diamonds—in French : *carreaux*—the two different names giving expression to exactly the same idea : that of the soul or *persona* of the spirit. The diamond is a jewel which allows the light to pass almost without any loss ; the purer its ' water ' the less the loss and the higher its value, which is the reason why Occultists call a perfected soul a ' Diamond-Soul.' The French and the Dutch use the same simile in a somewhat more prosaic though still very pretty way, when they compare the soul with a little window through which God is looking downstairs (Flemish : *vensterke*) into the lower worlds. The same is said of the human eye, which is styled the little window or *vensterke* of the soul in its turn. This is the origin of the French *carreaux* and the Dutch *ruiten*. Its symbolic figure is clear enough :

Without a shadow of doubt cups stand for diamonds or *carreaux* and for the element Water.

Ordinary divination correctly ascribes to cups the property of ruling money matters, because the soul is, in fact, the producer of work, which results in the production of ' money.'

The figure for diamonds in playing-cards is a square standing on one point, the opposite point reaching upwards. This symbolises the soul in its chief characteristic, standing on one end, one-pointedly directed towards Heaven or spirit and on the other hand one-pointedly directed towards Earth or matter, and squaring the Two within itself. One who really understands this may well be called a ' square man.'

SWORDS.—Not much choice is left with regard to the fourth suit or colour. Perhaps a sword looks more like a magic instrument than a spade, but both are made of iron, which ' cleaves ' the Earth or ' the body of Earth.'

When in the *Bhagavad Gîtâ*, the evident intention is to make it clear, that Shri Krishna did not appear in a ' body of Earth ' or physical body, one of the images used to express this meaning is : " weapons cleave Him not."

Originally the sword and spade had the same meaning. Compare the Spanish *espada* and the French *épée* for sword. A later meaning of ' spade ' became that of the agricultural tool.

In one way, viz. as a physical instrument, the emblem of executive power, the sword has much the same meaning as the wand or club : both are instruments of command, compelling obedience. The difference lies in the nature of the element used : wands compel by reason, intelligence, understanding, moral force ; swords enforce obedience to laws of Earth, material necessity, actual resistance. This means also, that wands open moral, intellectual and reasonable possibilities, swords give material opportunities.

Both these suits start from the First house or Aries, as will be worked out further hereafter, the one leading up from the beginning of Intelligence, the other from the beginning of activity in Matter.

The swords wound or even kill, they sever the rotten limb from the otherwise healthy body, for which reason the sword became the symbol for discrimination between practical usefulness and practical uselessness. From this, practical ideas of Right and Wrong, Good and Evil spring into being.

To wound and to kill is to destroy partially or wholly a body of Earth. This must not be regretted, as Shri Krishna explains, because it is only destroying *maya*, misleading appearances. That which is an inner reality can never be killed; it is Life itself. So the swords may mean destruction to some form or body, formula or limited existence, they may inflict pain, detriment, loss, sorrow upon bodily existence and material possessions or conditions. On the other hand they may mean renovation, birth and rebirth, the removing of obstacles, a clearance of the way and of the field of action, as the spade clears and turns the soil of the garden for a new sowing. So Jesus might well say : " I have not come to bring peace, but a sword." And even so, where the I or Self manifests in the world of outer phenomena, it will be obliged to take either the sword or the spade in hand to kill out wrongs, illusions, obstacles or turn the soil for a new sowing. Sometimes it may have to cut away what is not wanted, in order to keep the rest pure and straight and healthy ; just as the sculptor works on the marble. So also sorrow and pain will be inflicted upon the body of Earth so long as the hand of the Heavenly Sculptor is upon it.

The symbolic figure drawn for spades in playing-cards is the reverse of that for hearts, plus a design at the top reminding us of the cross upon the circle

in the symbol of the planet Mars : it appears also to signify something in the nature of the heart oppressed by the cross of matter.

That ordinary divination takes spades as malific as it makes hearts benefic, will be clear from the above.

From an inner standpoint it is not seen in the same way ; this also will be clear.

The colours of the spades and wands are always given as *black*, hearts and cups as *red*. The symbology of the Tarot is too pure for such a detail to be an accident, though the ordinary pack of playing-cards might be considered to some extent as a sort of ' profanation ' of the original Tarot. These colours, however, bear an essential meaning, as does everything in the Tarot.

Wands take their black colour from the ' Black Wisdom ' (compare the *Secret Doctrine*) ;

Swords or spades are black from the Earth, which has no light of its own ;

Hearts are coloured red by the ' blood ' and cups by the ' wine,' the liquor of life in the body and in the soul respectively, and both bearing light. So the Wine imparts the Holy Communion of the spirit to the soul, and the blood renders the same service, relatively, to the particles of the body, to which it imparts the life of the Ego or rather of its soul.

As I have explained in my previous book referred to above, Evolution may well be represented by a spiral starting from the spiritual centre and descending through the twelve houses of zodiacal ideation and formation into the ' worlds '—spiritual, psychical, physical.

This Spiral of Evolution may be divided into at least three parts, that is, three different beginnings may be seen. There is the Divine Beginning, starting in Aries, the sign of Initiation and highest abstraction, *the divine cycle* being completed in Pisces, where it is handed over or ' offered ' or sacrificed to the world of appearances.

The cycle of the spiritual in Man begins in the fifth sign, Leo, the *individual cycle* being that of the Spark or the Ego, and it runs from this sign of the heart to Cancer, the sign of memories.

Subsequently : a cycle of the personal being of the Ego, the cycle of the soul in Man, which we may call the *personal cycle*, starts from Sagittarius, the sign of thought and manifestation, and ends in Scorpio, the sign of death.

Then there is the *cycle of the body*, body of Earth, with the etheric initiative in Aries once more at the same point but lower down in the scale, and ending in Pisces as the house of the ' Universal Solvent,' applying also to the body of Earth, for here personal separateness is solved into the physical surroundings of the Universe from which it was built up.

After this the physical *organs in the body* of Earth will be built up and have their own cycle, starting again in Leo and building them between the heart and the stomach : Cancer.

And in Sagittarius the *physical manifestations* in happenings, deeds, facts, proceedings, etc., begin their cycle in co-operation with their surroundings. This cycle again ends in Scorpio, where life's lessons or experiences are drawn out of the materials.

Divine Intelligence being the beginning of all that to *our* conception means Evolution, the Spiral of Evolution must necessarily open with the suit of Wands, thus ruling the First to the Twelfth house. They stand for intelligence in general and ' intelligences ' in Nature, for messages and communications, relations, connections, plans and ideas, for knowledge and insight. They work through the head and have to do with ' mutations.'

Then follow hearts, representing the individual cycle, from the Fifth to the Fourth house. They rule in this cycle the fiery force of the spirit and represent power, goodness, love, fixed purpose, desire, well-being, virtue, warmth and heat, generation, development, they work through the heart.

The cups rule the cycle of the soul, or personal cycle, and represent, working from the Ninth to the Eighth house, the emotions and motives, the activity of the soul, its experiences from the highest philosophy and religion down to the merest lust or sensation. They work through the senses and the organs of motion.

They have what may be described as an undulating movement, and they may be favourable or unfavourable. But they move and cause growth and death, rise and decline ; they mould life into physical circumstances and forms ; they ' influence ' everything and this is their particular business.

The body of Earth is built up by the elements of Earth, represented by the suit of swords, running from the First house again up to the Twelfth. They speak of birth in matter, of facts, formations and resistance, of material good luck and bad fortune, achievements and failure in material respect ; of afflictions and pain, but also of the effects produced by this suffering.

Again comes the cycle of hearts, now in the significance of the round of physical organs. This is very strict and can be absolutely relied upon. Every astrologer can tell you the relationship between the houses and the organs of the body. But it must be borne in mind that this rulership first relates to the ethereal centres or chakras, the fiery wheels in the etheric body. So the Fifth house rules the solar plexus and the heart . . . etc.

Finally the cups rule the cycle of events, happenings, movements. From the Ninth to the Eighth house again.

In a general way the cups will relate to water, as the hearts to fire, the wands to air, and the spades to earth in the practice of daily life as well as in a philosophical sense.

It appears further that each of the three cycles come twice into play: the cycle of Aries—Pisces by wands and swords; that of Leo—Cancer by hearts on two different *niveaux*; and that of Sagittarius-Scorpio in the same way twice by cups.

Astrologers may wonder perhaps, how and why it is that the 'mutable' suits of wands and spades start from the 'moveable' sign Aries, while the 'moveable' suit of cups starts from the 'mutable' sign Sagittarius. We can only answer that the facts are as they are, but may add, that evidently every suit has something of a particular sort of accent, which does not necessarily fall on the first sign or house, but on that in which house and suit coincide with regard to element and property (*guna*). Thus:

Spades, earth and mutable, will have their accent in the sign Virgo, mutable sign of earth, in which discrimination is said to be born;

Cups, water and moveable, in the moveable sign of water Cancer, which in fact is the proper sign

of the moon and in which all properties of the
soul can be said to be gathered or hidden ;

Hearts, fire and fixed, in the fixed and fiery sign Leo ;
the suit of hearts appears to be the only one out
of the four to have its particular accent on the
first ' card ' or house, which naturally confirms
the essential being of hearts as interpreting fire
and the centre of things ;

Wands, air and mutable, have their accent on the airy
and mutable sign Gemini, the sign of the
Messenger.

The subsequent cycles are so many suits of Principles in the process of Building the Cosmos, Houses
in the Holy City of the Great Architect of the Universe. They represent happenings in the proceedings
of Evolution and experiences on the side of Involution
at the same time.

If the suits of colours in the Tarot system convey
any meaning at all, it must be this, and there cannot
be anything else to represent except these principles
and houses, happenings and experiences. We shall
see hereafter, how the Greater Arcana falls in with
them, and may now proceed to explain the rôle of
the Lesser Arcana.

Each suit of cards has been given as a set of *fourteen*,
viz. *ten* numbered cards, ace to ten, and four ' court
cards ' named King, Queen, Page or Knave, and
Knight. The latter has been omitted in the ordinary
playing-cards. Now whereas the cosmological cycle
consists of twelve houses, these sets or suits have ten
or fourteen cards—just as we choose to take it. Still—
if we take for granted—that the analogy exists, each
principle must be represented in a card and *vice*

versa. If it were not so, the Tarot system would be found wanting, and we have sufficient reasons not to accept this supposition beforehand, both by reason of theoretical and practical tests, the traditional renderings of the cards confirming the experience.

We need not trouble about the question *why* the Initiates, who presented the Western World with such an inheritance, chose to number up to ten only instead of going to Twelve. The ' Chosen People ' were given only *ten* commandments for their guidance. They who understand astrology in its essential meaning, can perceive something of the reason ; afterwards when the Preacher of Divine Life came to the same chosen people, He gave a double new commandment to complete the ancient Law : that of Brotherhood (Aquarius—eleven) and Love (Pisces—twelve).

In each suit of Tarot cards the numbering is from the one or ace up to the ten ; the King is to be considered in some way as a higher octave of the *one*, the Queen or Dame as the same of the *two*, whereas the Page or Knave is a representative of the ' relation between the two ' and consequently is a higher octave of *three*, while the Knight is the higher octave of the *four* and the other side of the same ' relation.' This absolutely covers the general and conventional meanings of Pages and Knights in the Tarot system and its divination, the Pages being said to be always something of messengers, and the Knights to be significs of transition, conversion, transmission, changing from one condition into another. But at the same time we find the intimation, that the Page as well as the Knight ' bears a double meaning.' Now, as they stand for ' the relation between the two ' they already bear an inherent

' double meaning ' or significance of a double nature. But ' double meaning ' implies something else and something more.

The Page and the Knight are also the figures standing for the XIth and XIIth principles, in the Eleventh and Twelfth houses, conveying the commandments of their King and Queen, as their messengers or officers, and at the same time standing as it were for the whole suit collectively, while in the former meaning, viz. as higher octaves of the 3 and 4, they are the messenger and bridge from one suit to the next one.

To give the analogy between the cards of the Tarot's Lesser Arcana and the zodiacal houses categorically :

WANDS :

1 and King	Aries	or	I house
2 „ Queen	Taurus	„	II „
3 „ Page	Gemini	„	III „
4 „ Knight	Cancer	„	IV „
5	Leo	„	V „
6	Virgo	„	VI „
7	Libra	„	VII „
8	Scorpio	„	VIII „
9	Sagittarius	„	IX „
10	Capricornus	„	X „
Page	Aquarius	„	XI „
Knight	Pisces	„	XII „

HEARTS :

1 and King	Leo	or	V house
2 „ Queen	Virgo	„	VI „
3 „ Page	Libra	„	VII „

c

HEARTS (*continued*):

4 and Knight		Scorpio	or	VIII	house	
5		Sagittarius	,,	IX	,,	
6		Capricornus	,,	X	,,	
7		Aquarius	,,	XI	,,	
8		Pisces	,,	XII	,,	
9		Aries	,,	I	,,	
10		Taurus	,,	II	,,	
	Page	Gemini	,,	III	,,	
	Knight	Cancer	,,	IV	,,	

CUPS :

1 and King		Sagittarius	or	IX	house	
2 ,, Queen		Capricornus	,,	X	,,	
3 ,, Page		Aquarius	,,	XI	,,	
4 ,, Knight		Pisces	,,	XII	,,	
5		Aries	,,	I	,,	
6		Taurus	,,	II	,,	
7		Gemini	,,	III	,,	
8		Cancer	,,	IV	,,	
9		Leo	,,	V	,,	
10		Virgo	,,	VI	,,	
	Page	Libra	,,	VII	,,	
	Knight	Scorpio	,,	VIII	,,	

SWORDS :

1 and King		Aries	or	I	house	
2 ,, Queen		Taurus	,,	II	,,	
3 ,, Page		Gemini	,,	III	,,	
4 ,, Knight		Cancer	,,	IV	,,	
5		Leo	,,	V	,,	
6		Virgo	,,	VI	,,	
7		Libra	,,	VII	,,	
8		Scorpio	,,	VIII	,,	

SWORDS (*continued*):

9		Sagittarius	or	IX house
10		Capricornus	,,	X ,,
	Page	Aquarius	,,	XI ,,
	Knight	Pisces	,,	XII ,,

A diagram of the Spiral of Evolution will be added with its suits of cards. It will be seen, that :

King, 1, 5, 9, fall on houses of Fire
Queen, 2, 6, 10 ,,   ,,   Earth
Page, 3, 7   ,,   ,,   Air
Knight, 4, 8,   ,,   ,,   Water

Astrologers will be able to draw immediate conclusions from these coincidences, which are absolutely natural.

One other detail may be added in this part :
The cards of the heart-suit must relate to *years*, to the day-time and summer, those of the cup-suit to *months*, to night-time and winter, the swords to *days* (in duration : i.e.—axial rotations of the Earth), while wands do not seem to have much relation to time and may consequently mean, that a thing will not happen at all, will remain in the realm of ideas, or is in the act of happening itself at the very moment. These particulars may be useful in the practice of divination.

Further, hearts relate to gold, cups to silver and to money in general, wands may relate to paper money and effects, shares, bonds, acts. Swords relate to material objects, and in general may indicate the cost or price of things, losses, debt, as well as the things bought by money.

In proportion to the more or less exoteric stand-point of the consulent and . . . the professor of divination, hearts will specially indicate ' good ' and ' yes,' spades ' bad ' and ' no,' while wands may mean ' indifferent, perhaps, doubtful, relatively, un-decided as yet,' and cups do not appear to confer any special meaning with relation to these things, except that they may make the feelings pervert the facts. They also give the sentiment with which the facts will be received or encountered.

Hearts are ' sunny ' and more or less venusian ; cups are jovial, sometimes neptunian, and may become ' loony ' in weak cases ; spades are martial and, by reflex, saturnian ; wands are mercurial and sometimes uranian.

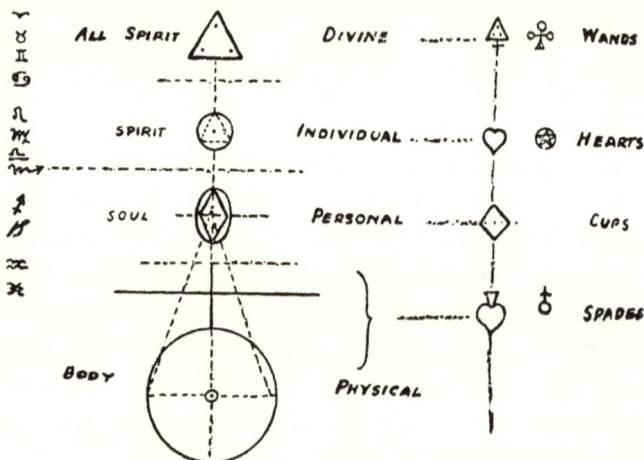

To conclude these considerations on the Lesser Arcana, it will be interesting to compare a general figure or diagram of the process of Creation with the four suits of the Tarot, and it will be seen that even the symbolic figures of our playing-cards are very distinctly to be recognised in it.

The four court-cards of each suit make together the full zodiac. When the soul reaches perfection, the oval form becomes a circle, and the nearer this state is approached, the more the two focal points of the ellipse draw together and the inscribed quadrangle approaches to the square.

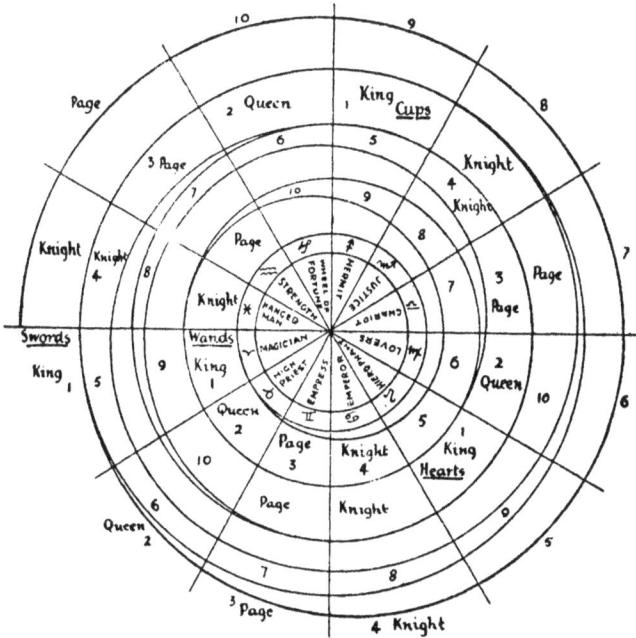

THE GREATER ARCANA

In the Greater Arcana competent authors on the subject have rightly seen a system of rendering or symbolising the great cosmic principles of Creation *per se*. Not in relation to any special plane or element but above these, and consequently to be considered as the abstract origin of all and everything in the Lesser Arcana.

Papus gives us the descriptions of the Greater

Arcana from the *Book of Hermes*, which probably will be the source *in concrete* of all later descriptions up to our time. How this book has been delivered through the ages is not known to me, but the clearness and systematic accuracy of these descriptions are proof of a high origin.

Where Papus, in his book on *The Tarot of the Bohemians* ventures to indicate relationship between the symbols of the Greater Arcana and zodiacal and planetary principles, he is hopelessly *wrong* however. He does not insist on it nor does he appear to make any use at all of these relations or explain *how* they are to be found out. Logic is entirely absent in this particular side of his renderings.

Without any difficulty or doubt we read in the first twelve arcanas the essential natures of the twelve zodiacal houses. Thus :

Arcana	I.	*The Magician* .	.	Aries
„	II.	*The High Priestess*	.	Taurus
„	III.	*The Empress* .	.	Gemini
„	IV.	*The Emperor* .	.	Cancer
„	V.	*The Hierophant*	.	Leo
„	VI.	*The Lovers* .	.	Virgo
„	VII.	*The Chariot* .	.	Libra
„	VIII.	*The Justice* .	.	Scorpio
„	IX.	*The Hermit* .	.	Sagittarius
„	X.	*The Wheel of Fortune*		Capricornus
„	XI.	*The Strength* .	.	Aquarius
„	XII.	*The Hanged Man*	.	Pisces

We do not know what sort of conclusions Dr. Papus and others may have drawn for themselves, but it seems rather astonishing that this analogy has never been stated in public. It is as easy to recognise the nine planetary principles, i.e. those at present known to astronomy and astrology, in the following arcanas. So we find :

Arcana	XIII.	Death .	.	.	Saturn
,,	XIV.	Temperance .		.	Mercury
,,	XV.	The Devil	.	.	Mars
,,	XVI.	The Tower	.	.	Uranus
,,	XVII.	The Star	.	.	Venus
,,	XVIII.	The Moon	.	.	Moon
,,	XIX.	The Sun	.	.	Sun
,,	XX.	The Last Judgment			Jupiter
,,	XXI.	The World	.	.	Neptune

while :

Arcana XXII or Zero : the Fool must evidently be taken for the principle of the Earth itself, upon which we are carried away in space without being able to loose ourselves from its course. It may be as well interpreted as the *Pars Fortunae,* which must not be mistaken for the ' Wheel of Fortune ' in the series of the arcanas. This has as much to do with the former as the cusp of the Tenth house has in the horoscope with the *Pars Fortunae.*

We shall treat everyone of these cards in its turn hereafter. First let us have the scheme at large.

THE METHOD OF DIVINATION

In the same way as the Chinese Book *I-Ging* originally was edited or taught as a book of wisdom and insight into universal principles and stages of being and becoming, happenings in the eternal process of evolution in the nature of the world and of men, so the beautiful pictures of the Tarot system are a teaching of wisdom and insight into the process of world-creation. Divination is a practice or practical use of the universal system in a particular instance. And so the universal may elucidate the particular and throw light down in the world of phenomena, darkly veiled by the maya of matter. How divination works will remain for ever a mystery to the profane. But it does. And though the unseen intermediary belongs most certainly to the angelic order, the system will work even where the visible professor or medium of divination is anything but an angel. Only . . . the interpretation given by the latter is what makes the literal divination. And this may be more or less esoteric or exoteric.

There are many different methods of laying out the cards for the purpose of divination. The aim is always to get the cards to show, by means of their universal symbolism, what the actual circumstances and other actualities in the consultant's case are. To reach this aim, the consultant is made to shuffle the cards so that they are mixed by *his* hands, and the way they mix will naturally condition the laying out. In doing this, the consultant himself is denoted by some or other card, and the surrounding cards, which are laid according to some accepted scheme, will give his relations to facts and persons in his surroundings. So it is said. And many systems work well, according to their adherents.

Now when we dispose of a system so complete and logical as that of the horoscope, how could we indicate better the relations of a given personality to his surroundings than by means of the twelve houses, which show every relation possible ? Then why not use this scheme, ready for action ? This was the present author's starting point. The system he worked out upon this horoscopic basis (and it works with astonishing accuracy) runs as follows :

The Greater Arcana, constituting the macrocosmic principles, must be always used entirely. The Lesser Arcana will appear only partially in every particular instance, as only twice thirteen cards are used out of fifty-six.

Divide the cards of the former into two packs : the twelve zodiacal and the ten other cards, planets and Fool.

Take the pack of zodiacal cards of the Greater Arcana and let the consultant shuffle it well and at his ease. When he has got the impression that it will do, lay them out in a circle as the twelve houses of the horoscope, starting from I by II, III . . . etc. This circle is the base for all later judgment of the figure obtained, because it contains the principal lines of the whole ; the consultant's radical essentials as well as his present individual conditions. The latter predominate more or less, but when you have a consultant for the first time, you will not have to ask him for his birth date even to be able to say much about his character, temperament, etc., and about his present state of mind. These twelve houses of the Greater Arcana give you pretty well a direct impression of the nativity combined with the principal progressive features, up to date. It may be stated here, that the Intelligences, working through cards and other methods of divination, are also indicated by the suit of wands.

After having laid out the twelve houses with the cards of the Greater Arcana, let him take the pack of the Lesser Arcana and shuffle it well, taking his time over it easily, in order to impose his own will (or magnetism, as some prefer to put it) on the cards. When he gets the impression that it is enough, he may still cut them twice or thrice, as he likes. Then lay them out : beginning to take the cards from the top and following the houses as before : I, II, III, etc. . . . After the first circle is thus laid, put the thirteenth card on the centre. Then lay a second circle in the same way and again the thirteenth card on the centre. The rest of the pack is laid aside and remains out of the figure. But do not change their order, because in some cases there may be use for one or two more cards.

The second circle now indicates the forces or activities working in the consultant himself in connection with his surroundings and *vice versa*. The accent lies here on the Self and the side of his own decision. In the third circle we find rather the forces and activities working in the surroundings in connection with the consultant himself, and the accent of this circle lies rather on the Not-self and on destiny. The cards in the third circle must be read generally in the way that is called ' reversed ' in card divination.

It is difficult, however, to tell exactly how each case will work out and in what way it must be read. Divination is an art, and to become an artist in it one must be born an artist first and practise well to develop one's spiritual inheritance. One cannot learn everything by reading books, nor can an author explain everything he has found by his own experience.

Cards may indicate persons in particular or certain categories of persons, they may relate to Intelligences and elementary forces, working in the karma

of the consultant. As a matter of fact the cards
laid out for divination have always the meaning of
a picture of the effects of karma, detailed and re-
corded up to the actual moment, but containing at
the same time much of the past and certain prognosis
on the other hand. It takes a long time and serious
application to draw out everything contained in a
card figure.

The cards may stand for things and objects and
facts, and indicate time, duration, circumstances.
The less dogmatic one is with regard to the process
of divination and its interpretation, the greater the
chance of being truly ' illuminated ' by insight or
vision. These cards have to be taken as ' signs of
the Heavens,' and in order to understand what
Heaven has to communicate, man has to eliminate,
wholly and without consideration, his own as well
as other prople's prejudices and preferences, bigotry
and illusions. Pessimism and optimism are both
false and of no use in facing the natural facts, though
we shall do wisely not to disregard the free-choice
(wrongly called : free-will), as in the horoscope
and its interpretation. This spiritual *libre arbitre*,
however, must equally be indicated by the cards,
and will moreover always have to work with the
conditions given and indicated by the rest of the
cards.

When the three circles have been laid, the consultant should take and shuffle the remaining planetary cards of the Greater Arcana, including the Fool,
and may now himself choose in which houses to
place them. Of course it is essential that these
should remain covered till all are disposed of. You
may place more than one card in a house, just as

there may be more than one planet in one house of the horoscope. So, if a matter appears to you to be of extraordinary importance, place two or three cards upon the house ruling the matter. If the consultant thinks it difficult and cannot make his choice as to the places of the planetary cards, let his hand hover over the figure and place the cards at hazard. Then generally this ' hazard ' will prove remarkably accurate and well informed. For the rest, personal thinking must be as little to the fore as possible in these proceedings, as it is not so ' divine ' as to help much in the act of divination proper. Everybody can learn in a few moments the way of laying out the cards whatever the system may be. But very few people succeed in the right interpretation, even with the use and profit of the formulated rendering of different authors—Papus, Waite, Mathers, etc.

The purely astrological method presented in this essay, working with the original Tarot system, offers—we dare to say—the best opportunity of reading every detail, as well as the cardinal points in the consultant's karma at the moment of judging.

If after the judgment there remain definite questions unanswered or vague, and the consultant ardently desires a ' yes ' or a ' no,' he may take the remaining pack of cards of the Lesser Arcana, turn the card on top of it, lay it on the house relating to the question and consider this as the most definite answer possible for the moment.

One must not expect to have all questions answered positively at every moment. It is absolutely certain, that one does *not* get everything answered. There never was an oracle that answered all questions. This may be contrary to the spirit of Western scientific thought, but the fact is as I have stated. And after all why should it be contrary to real scientific thought at all, if we consider the Intelligences referred to as beings, as conscious of their duty and responsibility as, let us say, the best of us men.

The two cards on the middle represent some sort of a synthesis of karmic conditions and events at the actual moment, or something predominating.

Practising this system we have had opportunity of observing that facts that are certain and of such importance as to dominate the conditions of the consultant in some way, are always indicated more than once. Sometimes even as often as three or four times in the same figure. This after all is not strange, because in an astrological figure the houses are closely related and important things always affect more than one factor in a man's conditions. So some strong feature must necessarily appear more than once in a figure of such a familiar interdependence.

To read a card-figure laid on this scheme some elementary knowledge of astrology is desirable. We cannot enter here into any further astrological explanation specifically, and would refer our readers to the literature on the point.

In the next part, however, we hope to explain the significance of the cards sufficiently for the use of divination.

SIGNIFICANCE OF THE CARDS

THE GREATER ARCANA

THE significance of the cards—Greater as well as Lesser Arcana—as it has been delivered through the ages, is often remarkably accurate, as far as can be verified. In what way, however, it has come down to us, and what reasonable ground there may be for the given meanings, remain mysteries, not to be elucidated by the present author. By verification we mean theoretical consideration on the basis both of astrological systematics and of the practice of divination. The fact is, that the traditional significance is generally in accordance with the astrological explanation of the cards as we have given it here, though this explanation has not yet been offered by any author before, as far as we know. So we may conclude, that this key has been lost or has been hidden from those who kept the practice alive and left the system to us.

In the following pages we shall give the meaning of both Greater and Lesser Arcana after the astrological theory expounded by us, together with a short résumé of the traditional significance, the latter taken chiefly from Papus and from the renderings of Mr. Waite. For the sake of shortness and simplicity we shall mark our quotations with *P* for Papus, *W* for A. E. Waite, *M* for S. L. MacGregor Mathers.

I. *The Magician. Aries.*

The first sign or house in the Zodiac is the first step in the direction of Manifestation, and Aries is the High Priest as well as Avidya or Ignorance, standing before, c.q. above cognition. Potency and power are its attributes, because all and everything is immanent in this stage of Beginning. Power abstract, undeveloped, simple, but for that reason mightier than every detail or phenomenon, and the master of Nature. The ultra-positive, the very superior, and in the lower human sense the ultra-egotistical. Like the first note of a composition in music, it determines the tone and gives the key. From the First spring the Four, and so the symbols of the Four Elements appear on the table of the Magician, though his action, as far as action goes in this card and principle, exists in potency only and is indicated consequently in the wand in his right hand. In his superior abstractness he is eternal in relation to the phenomenal world, which is indicated by the symbols of Eternity above his head, the *lemnescate,* and around his waist, the serpent.

W.: " This card signifies the divine motive in man, reflecting God, the will in the liberation of its union with that which is above."

M.: "He symbolises *Will.*"—This is exactly Aries.

P.: " The Unity principle, the origin of which is impenetrable to human conceptions, is placed at the beginning of all things." His upright attitude indicates " the will that is going to proceed into action."

The First house or Ascendant gives the key-note of the physical self, reflection of the Higher Self, and thus in the practice of divination the Magician denotes the consultant, personally. In every figuration of cards it is further the 'beginning' and initiative.

As far as we may ascribe siderial meanings to the cards of the Greater Arcana, the Magician should rule the month of Aries, i.e. from the 21 March to 20 April. It appears gravely doubtful, however, if this may be considered to determinate incidental occurrences in time. It will certainly relate to properties of the sign Aries in general and in particular and consequently owned by people born between those dates. But for the rest definition of time, date or hour must be sought in the cards of the Lesser Arcana, as far as we know.

II. *The High Priestess. Taurus.*

The second stage in macrocosmic evolution is the polarity of the omnipotent might of Self, omnipotent possibility of the field of manifestation, universal passive richness, the *Kamaduk* or Most Beloved Wish-Cow of the Hindus. This macrocosmic field is the Temple of the Great Magician or Architect, in potency at least. It is the Bull, Taurus, of astrology, the house of sound, art, faith and richness. To speak truly, it is not so much sound as the principle of the soundbox, sound itself having its origin in the next step. Therefore Papus may well compare this card with the hieroglyphic meaning of the Hebrew letter *Beth*, which relates to " the mouth of man as the organ of speech." But it is *not* " God the Son " as he says elsewhere. It might be called ' God the Woman,' the Divine Mother, the ' Eternal Feminine.' As the passive richness of the Universe awaiting him that will be able to see it and appreciate it, this principle may well be symbolised by the image of the High Priestess, sitting in an attitude of waiting, between the pillars of the Temple, *B* and *J*, standing for the *Two*, from which will spring the worlds of spirit and of matter. Being Supreme Objectivity, it is the symbol of receiving, of possessing, of cult and adoration. It symbolises womanhood in general, as the first card symbolised manhood.

Mr. Waite has restored in his images the original picture of Isis, reposing on the crescent moon, which indeed I should say must be regarded as the best representative of the goddess of Taurus, in which sign the moon is ' exalted,' as astrology teaches. But Isis is not so much to be regarded as representing " Science, Wisdom, Knowledge " (*M*.)—as the goddess " of Nature, whose veil must not be raised before the profane." (*P*.) and of supreme consciousness, because ' consciousness ' is the faculty committed by Earth.

W. calls her " Second Marriage of the Prince " and says, that in divination she stands for the querent if female. Now I should say, this cannot be altogether true, as in the horoscope the first house indicates the personal temperament, etc., for a man as well as for a female querent. So in cards the Magician must always bear the meaning of the querent personally, but if a female she will be largely influenced by the High Priestess, as this is the representative of the feminine in general and female properties. It may be true, more or less, that for a man this card represents " the woman who interests the querent " (*W*.), just as on the other hand the Magician represents the man who interests the querent if this happens to be a woman.

D

The High Priestess symbolises constancy, fidelity, repose, stability, but also dumbness, laziness, resistance, endurance as well as passive opposition. It rules everything in connection with art and the artistic abilities, with wealth and with the masonic lodge.

III. *The Empress. Gemini.*

If the Hebrew letter *Gimel* means the throat (as a canal for sound) and also " the hand of man half closed in the act of prehension " (*P.*), then it may indeed well stand for the house of Gemini as for no one else ; because Gemini is the macrocosmic ' relation between the two ' which is potential vibration, symbolised by ' sound,' and this sign rules the hands of man, with which he grips this relation actually. It rules the ' Word, which was with God in the beginning ' and words, speech and correspondence in this world below, as above. It means cognisance, from which science may spring later, but it is not science itself. Nor is it ' action ' (*M.*), though it is the origin of, sometimes the pretext for, activity. But it includes indecision, uncertainty, doubt, change, intercourse, reflection, appearance and everything that the sign Gemini may further communicate.

This Empress is indeed " a daughter of Heaven and Earth " (*W.*), for she represents the sphere of Mercury, Messenger of the Gods, and so this card always bears the meaning of messages and writing, and of news to be heard, instructions to be received. Twelve (in older pictures nine) stars are placed around her head and this certainly means that down here on earth the messages come to us from the stars, a gentle hint at astrology. We regret that in the picture of *W.*, the wings, with which the figure is gifted, and the shield with eagle in her right hand, as shown in older editions of this card have been omitted, for both hold a due indication of the element Air. Gemini is the first house of Air, and sound uses the air as its medium. The use of the sign of Venus is not very clear in the picture given by *W.* because it is not Venus but Mercury that rules the house of the Empress. One of the older editions shows the Empress holding in her left hand a wand with a heraldic lily, a sort of trefoil on its top, very suggestive of the origin of the colour or suit of Wands, which of course has a close relation with the card of Gemini.

Why this idea of the messenger is drawn as a woman, and given the name of the ' Empress ' is very well explained by Mr. *W.* in these words : " because there is no direct message which has been given to man like that which is borne by woman." Woman rules the world. As a mother she is the ' canal ' by which the human being is conducted from another world into this one, and as a female she attracts the man, in order to ' double ' herself and to impart a double value to life on earth. This is indicated in the image of the Twins, originally Adam-Eve destined to be united by Knowledge. This is the card of Knowledge.

Also of ' universal fecundity ' as *W.* has it.

IV. *The Emperor. Cancer.*

There is much more mystery buried in every symbol than words spoken can tell. Superficial consideration might make astrologers wonder at this image, which assimilates worldly power with the sign Cancer instead of with Leo, to which they are accustomed. Still there remains this to be taken into account, that originally ' emperors ' got their power *from the people*,—China, Rome—long before they began to claim God as their private protector against eventual aggression from outside. The people are ruled by the sign of Cancer, says the astrologer. And thus originally the chosen emperor accepted *vox populi* as *vox Dei*. This chosen dignitary was nothing of a tyrant, originally, nor did he have anything to do with rulership or warfare : he was simply the highest and most pure expression of the soul of the people or nation. In China sometimes a poor but extremely virtuous old man without any other antecedents was elected to be emperor. All later usurpations of power and succession were deviations from the old and pure institution. The present position of the president in a republic comes very near to that of the original emperor.

The sign of the soul indeed is . . . Cancer. At the same time this is the sign of the breast (*P.*) and of the womb, as *W.* translates this passage about the card, which *P.* says is connected with the Hebrew letter *Daleth*. In the older pictures we see the effort to let the man make a figure 4 or something like the symbol for Jupiter with his crossed legs. There may be some meaning in it, but this seems futile with regard to the general significance of the Emperor as the representative of the past, of memory, tradition in the people and in family life, dharma and the real motives of the soul in the background of life, which actually rule life. It relates.to every inner power of the soul from which outer activity (karma) will arise.

In different editions of the cards we find different sorts of sceptres in the hand of the Emperor. In some there appears also an eagle. We prefer the sceptre which Mr. *W.* puts into his hands : the *crux ansata*, symbol of the might of inner life, which rules matter. The planet Jupiter has only to do with this card, in so far as it is exalted in the sign Cancer, which means, that virtually hopes and expectations as well as ideals for the future take their origin in the deep-rooted attachments of the soul, which themselves are the expression of dharma or cosmic memory.

Still in a personal way the Emperor indicates the father of the querent, because it is from his father that his soul derives its elements. Compare in the horoscope the IVth house. Therefore this seemingly very feminine sign was symbolised by a male figure, while the seemingly male messenger was represented by a woman. The Empress indicates the spiritual parentage, the Emperor the physical one. The latter finds its counterpart (physical mother) in the Xth house, as is well known.

Some authors say this card means ' realisation.' That is correct so far as this word means an inner realising of the significance of outer facts : the gathering of the harvest of experience, which will become the store of memory.

V. *The Hierophant. Leo.*

The fifth step on the cosmic ladder is that of the Atma, the Spark in macrocosmos and that of childbirth and of the heart in particular on the physical plane. The latter is sanctified by the former and this fact is symbolised in the image of the Hierophant.

It may also be interpreted in its turn as the sancti-fying of the profane (man) by the holy (man) in general, and this fact gave the reason for the other nomination of this card : *the pope*. Of course it may equally well be called the patriarch. In the masonic lodge it is the R.W.M., the sun in the solar system and the heart in every living body, as also the solar plexus in the etheric body. And as the teaching of St. Paul—and others—has it : from the heart are the issues into life. It is the dynamic centre of every living existence.

The Hierophant " is seated between the two pillars of Hermes and of Solomon " . . . " He is symbol of mercy and beneficence." (*M*.) This is exact. *P*. says he is the principle " which attaches the material body to the divine spirit." Which is pre-cisely that of the heart. So there remains little doubt with regard to identity. The same author identifies further the principle of the Hierophant with the Hebrew letter *He*, which means aspiration or breath. In fact the heart is the cause of this periodical move-ment, which we find in pulsation and respiration, in analogy with the Law of Periodicity in Cosmos.

In the different versions given by authors there is very little of value. The Hierophant is, in short; the heart and herein resides the motoric force for good or for evil, according to the more or less sancti-fying force that comes through. In case of affliction there may be lack of courage, self-confidence, honesty, sometimes certain evil or bad character.

It is rightly asserted, that this card may denote " the man to whom the querent has recourse " (*W*.), also some authority or official having power to sanc-tify or gratify demands. Leo is the ' king,' it is said by astrologers. And in mundane evolution the king derived his power from the emperor, as in the zodiac. He was invested by the latter with a power to wield and rule a definite and concrete organisation, for which he became individually responsible. So where the emperor was chosen and came forth from the soul of the people and apparently from below, the king is appointed from above, and seems more spiritual because more actually known. There ought to be no kings, however, without an emperor over them. The king is and remains the central official, as the heart is the central organ of the organism.

The triple crown of the Hierophant and his triple crossed staff both indicate his rulership in the three worlds, which I should like to name the spiritual, the psychical and the physical.

Some say the card means marriage. This may be, but only in the inner sense of true revelation to the heart, and consequently in the same sense as Jesus meant when He said : " Marriages are contracted in Heaven."

In another way, in practical divination, the card means of course ' sanction,' be it of marriage or of something else, but always in the way of inner consent, not of outer law, which is ruled by another house.

Self-centredness and some sort of natural authority are the chief characteristics of Leo and the Hierophant.

VI. *The Lovers. Virgo.*

From the original meaning of the sign Virgo, the virgin matter of the cosmos or world-ether, to that principle which makes ' lovers ' is rather a long step, but we will observe that all these Tarot symbols relate to human points of view and human life in particular, i.e. cosmic principles seen from this particular standpoint which gives more of a practical image than of abstract reasoning, the abstract cosmic significance, however, being imbedded fairly accurately in them. So in the human constitution the sign Virgo means the nervous system and everything acting as an organ as well as the relatively ' virginal matter ' which is extracted from the food and will serve to build up the body. So this house is known to rule health and sickness. It is further known to relate to the principles and materials of our work. And so the card of the Lovers must in the first place symbolise these things. It does indeed. *P.* says it is connected with the Hebrew letter *Vau* in its significance of " the eye, and all that relates to light and brilliancy. The eye establishes the link between the external world and ourselves ; by it light and form are revealed to us." In fact ' the eye ' is a very ancient symbol for the idea of ' organ ' ; the Neoplatonists repeatedly used it. When saying it " establishes the link," we must be aware, however, that it is not yet this link itself but offers the elements for it. And again this card does not say ' love ' but ' lovers ' (in the French edition of the cards the singular is used : *l'amoureux*). Evidently the meaning is this : what makes man feel ' amorous ' is his sensuousness, the word used in the strictly philosophical and biological meaning of receptivity of the senses for agreeable, caressing, benefic, gratifying vibrations. The same receptivity, however, exists on the other hand for disagreeable, painful, disturbing, malific vibrations. The receptivity and the condition of

an organic centre in its double possibility of experience is only the phenomenal expression of the same
in organic existence in general, consequently stamping
the whole of manifestation with the law of duality
of ' good ' and ' evil.' The latter is well illustrated
by the picture on the older cards where a youth is
represented standing between two women, the one
appearing to be benefic, the other malific. This
sensuousness indeed can lead to a lower sensuality
or can be the means of demonstrating love. A sort
of angelic figure (Cupid ?) is seen shooting an arrow :
symbol of the ray of light. The card which was
drawn on the authority of Mr. W. shows a man and
a woman in a state of paradisical nudity, and over
the two hovers the figure of an angel. It confers
much the same meaning, of course. " This is in all
simplicity the card of human love, here exhibited
as part of the way, the truth and the life." (W.) And
we shall find, that the same force which makes us
love, physically, is at the back of all the work we do.
Because it is the material response to the fiery and
central pushing power and includes actual possibility
on the basis of practical knowledge, experimental
knowing. W. did well to show the Tree of Knowledge
in the drawing, it being the symbol of Nature in general
and of the seed or seminal elements.

VII. *The Chariot. Libra.*

In the Seventh house of the evolutionary cycle the
relation of the Self with the Not-self or outer world
is contracted and completed and the ' organism '
arises as the systematic whole of organs, a lawful
microcosm, which in every instance is a phenomenon
of the Cosmic Law, first significance of Libra. This

idea is very well illustrated by the picture of the Chariot, drawn by the White and the Black Sphinx and governed by the Magician incarnate. It is the Self embodied. This card consequently means marriage, contract, body and bodily existence, organisation, achievement, co-operation.

P. says this card has to do with the Hebrew letter *Zain*, which " represents an arrow." Now it is very curious to see, that in Hindu astrology the sign Libra is symbolised by an arrow touching an eye, evidently meaning the principles of the organism or systematic complex of organs, and at the same time the understanding, or knowing, which is the result of the eye *seeing* the light.

The Magician has become the ' Conqueror ' ; the forces of good and of evil both drawing his chariot symbolise the fact that good and evil, agreeable as well as painful experiences, make us wiser and contain the elements of Existence, spirit and matter both.

As a matter of fact the card may have to do with our adversaries.

On the front " we see the Indian *lingam*," says *P.* we should like to add : in connection with the Indian (!) *yoni*, i.e. the union of the sexes, or the two in one (bond). Here the ' Fall ' into matter has been completed. The sphinxes are female entities, the driver of the Chariot is a man. This not only symbolises the subjugation of Nature by will-power, but also the fact that, while inwardly ' woman rules the world ' (the Empress), rulership in the outer world lies with man, and it is his duty to keep within due bonds the ' attractive ' forces of woman, who, however, appears to be the personification of motoric force to him and his ' chariot.' That woman practically gives the inspirational lead and motive to man in this world is being openly recognised by psychologists in our time.

VIII. *Justice. Scorpio.*

Whosoever might hesitate before the emblems of this card and think it might as well stand in relation with Libra on account of the idea of 'justice,' generally ascribed to the latter sign, and the balance which the woman holds in her left hand, will do well to consider the systematic relationship existing between all signs of the zodiac or evolutionary cycle. The left hand derives from, while the right hand is instrumental in giving out. Scorpio derives from Libra the balance and the idea of justice, but the sword in the right hand shows, that we have not justice pure and simple, platonic so to speak, but that which has often been called ' avenging justice.' *Au fond* it is more vengeance than justice and Scorpio is famous for its tendency to vengeance, in every way and every form. After Libra, the stage of total manifestation, this stage is the taking-back, the first step on the way home, which explains the well-known feature of desire, thirst for experience in this sign, because it wishes to bring home something from the voyage ' westward.' So the card of justice means above all the faculty of desire, higher as well as lower, from the most spiritual or religious longing down to the most crude lust. Sexual experience is one of the most important expressions of it, and we may safely say, that one of the principal significances of the card is sex. Another, principally where sex is sublimated, is occult experience, and the psychical side of earth-life in general. Naturally it stands in

close relation to the sign Virgo, on the other hand
of the Balance, in which sensation was born ; the
faculty (or possibility) of the sensation bringing the
desire to realise it. It is the sign of transmutation,
which is the change of the inner composition by the
experience won. The sensation realised makes one
feel, actually, bodily, psychically or morally, the
meaning of good and evil, and therefore the ' sword
of discrimination ' is the emblem in the right hand
of this figure. Every mistake in the process of life
will avenge itself with geometrical certainty. This
house is the school of life and it is remarkable how
it is concerned with ' school ' in every respect. In
this house the Self takes from life and from the cosmos surrounding what it wants, consequently what
it does not yet possess, and the card of Justice becomes
the index for our debts or the possessions of other
people.

Meanwhile the balance in the left hand of the
figure denotes, without the slightest doubt, that
since Libra is on the left hand Justice must be the
VIIIth card, *not* the XIth as some authors have it.

P. identifies this principle with that of the Hebrew
letter *Heth,* which " expresses a field, from it springs
the idea of anything that requires labour, trouble,
effort." The sexual union has taken place and
Adam-Eve are condemned to " earn their bread in
the sweat of their face " on the field. To say it less
tragically the divine gift of the senses obliges us to
work with them and to suffer by them as well as to
benefit by the enjoyment of their impressions.

It is the card of sorrow as well as of deeper satisfaction. In the man under this card there is always
something of the ' avenger of wrongs,' and very often

it has to do with the proceedings of justitia in the world. It is also the card of the secret, or hidden.

Most authors are not very famous for their interpretation of this card, but P. says a very good thing about it : " The sword here is a sign of protection for the good, as well as a menace for the bad."

IX. *The Hermit. Sagittarius.*

P.: " Humanity fulfilling the function of God the Holy Spirit. The human creative force." Indeed this is clearly Sagittarius for every astrologer. The author might have mentioned in the same line that the Hierophant (Leo) represents God the Son.

The Hebrew letter " *Thet* represents a roof and suggests the idea of safety and protection . . . protection ensured by wisdom." The astrologer says : the Ninth house is the house of the Master—idea of wisdom and protection in one ; the Master in fact shields his disciples like a roof . . . in some way.

The sign is that of thought-power, creative mind, idealism, which throw their own light on the things below, and consequently the Sagittarian is remarkable for always seeing things in his own light and trying to throw light on things in order to instruct other people. He is the eternal traveller, the indefatigable walker. And mentally he is always more or less lonely. All this is very distinctly symbolised in the card of the Hermit, which stands for ideas, perspectives, spiritual or moral influences and for light thrown upon the objects of this earth-life. In divination it stands for teachers, legal authorities, advisers and guides, and with the guiding principles in everything and questions, in relation to the querent.

But above all it is his own idealism, etc. The direction in which his thoughts are running.

In the older cards the Hermit is shielding his light on one side with his mantle. This may be indicative of the habit of Sagittarians to evade and disarm contradiction beforehand, knowing by intuition the power of darkness. He is leaning on the staff of knowledge with regard to earthy matters.

W. is perfectly right in saying, that " Prudence is the least of its meanings and the most negligible." Some authors (*M.*) held this card to be the symbol of ' prudence,' but indeed the Sagittarian is not very famous for this virtue, though the card is truly Sagittarian and nothing else. This is again proved by the striking explanation of *W.* : " His beacon intimates that ' where I am, you also may be.' " This is the stereotyped way in which a Sagittarian thinks.

X. *The Wheel of Fortune. Capricorn.*

" It symbolises *Fortune*, good or bad." (*M.*) So this means happenings, facts. It is indeed in the Tenth house, that the relation between the Self and the Not-self crystallises into fact, happening, deed. Says *P.*, identifying this card with the significance of the Hebrew letter *Yod*, that it indicates " the finger of man ; the forefinger extended as a sign of command." This clearly has to do with the significance of the Tenth house as that of authority and authorities, who are qualified to give commandments. The commandment itself comes under the same resort. " This letter has therefore become the image of potential (ל) manifestation, of spiritual duration and, lastly, of the eternity of time." In fact, the Tenth house of the zodiacal cycle, ruled by Saturn, has much to do with Time and manifestation in time, but not only potential ; real as well.

The image for this idea is very characteristic, perhaps the most striking of all. " The wheel of fortune suspended upon its axis. (Leaving no doubt about the idea of circular movement in time, which we find back in the horoscope.) To the right *Anubis*, the genius of good ascending ; to the left *Typhon*, the genius of evil descending . . ." (*P*.) See the right hand as the East and the left hand as the West, and you have the illustration of the horoscope more accurately still. As we know the East is standing for the source of spiritual force and inspiration, the West for the end of it and dying out.

What the sphinx has to do with it seems doubtful, unless it means that all mysteries will be revealed in time. The symbols of the four fixed signs are holding the four quarters of the card. The four fixed principles are indeed generally accepted as the basis of the material or concrete world. Compare the visions of Ezechiel and St. John of Patmos.

The mid-heaven in the horoscope sees the eastern half of it rising and the western half on the other hand declining.

The divinatory meanings of this card are evident : it denotes the authorities to which the querent is subject, but also his own actions, deeds, manifestations and the position in the world which he occupies, his name and titles. It is the card of karma in the strict sense and that which is indicated by it in divination will come true or be realised actually. Therefrom it has been said to symbolise ' fortune.' As will be seen it must not be accepted as the ' part of fortune ' in the horoscope, because this has a more specific meaning and only with regard to the moon.

It is the point where you get at the world or the world gets at you. It is 'ripe karma' above all, facts which are not to be overborne by words. The fruits of former thoughts.

XI. *Strength. Aquarius.*

The astrologer says, that the Eleventh house is the house of the ' friends.' This means, that it contains those who are with us, and that which we have within the limit of our power, because ' friendly,' is that which is understood. The forces of nature, which we have mastered, are friendly to us and this is very well expressed by the woman who " is closing the jaws of a lion." The latter stands for passion more particularly. She derives this force from the eternal or superhuman and this is indicated by the lemnescate above her head. In older editions of the card we find half the symbol for Aquarius, as a line of vibration added to it : ⌣. Viewed from a purely astrological standpoint it is evident, that the force to conquer Leo should be found in the opposite sign, Aquarius. Early Renaissance must have seen this in the same way, as we find exactly the same image—only with one difference : it is there a young man, not a woman—a man closing the jaws of a lion in the capital of a pillar in the church of St. Andrew-the-Less in Vienna. Which proves at the same time, that the chosen image is not of a very recent date. (*Musée du Trocadéro :* Paris.)

P. identifies it with the Hebrew letter *Kaph*, which he says " is a reinforcement of the *Gimel*—(Gemini)— so that we might say that it designates the hand of man in the act of grasping strongly. Ideas of strength are therefore applied to this letter." We should say it is the grip of friendship. A well-known symbol in many societies of brotherhood consisted of two hands united in a close grip of friendship.

" It is connected with the mystery of union . . . in all planes . . ." (*W*.), and this also is evident, because we are united with that which we have mastered and with people who are able to respond to our (electric) emanations of thought, or to whose emanations we ourselves respond.

XII. *The Hanged Man. Pisces.*

This twelfth sign of house, closing the cycle of the zodiac, means loss to the outer world, solution, handing over the results of one cycle to the following one, whence comes the meaning of treachery in common astrology. This house contains the things which we have not yet mastered and those whom we have failed to understand or who have failed to understand us. So either this remains for the next cycle, or it will tempt us to waste our last forces. In the eyes of the world it is the sign of waste, spoil, mishap. Viewed from the other side it is the sign of the *Golem*, in which the outer world loses its importance or even reality, and the consciousness is opened to inner truth. This is the reversing of consciousness, which makes things change their significance in such a way that they appear to turn upside down : the world is now viewed from the other side. And this is the significance of the hanged man.'

It is also the sign of Judas, who, as far as the outer world is able to judge, did not understand the signifi-

E

cance of Jesus and handed Him over to His enemies, the most mysterious of the disciples and apparently the fiend within the circle. What, however, is his treason or despair when viewed from the other side ? It is an act of ' perversion,' the result of human nature being too weak to carry on in this world the heavy load of spiritual revelation ; or even a mystic message, which till now has never been understood and will never be understood by the profane world. However this may be, we may feel pretty sure, that none of the others who remained in this world to preach the Gospel understood or, let us say rather, underwent the Message like Judas, who hanged himself.

Well may *W.* say : " It is a card of profound significance, but all the significance is veiled." Perhaps we might even add : it is the symbol of the veil itself and of everything that is and remains veiled in this world, and, in divination, to the querent, *ad hoc.*

P. tries to identify the Hanged Man with the Hebrew letter *Lamed* which " designates the arm " . . . but fails utterly in his effort to explain this. We should say, if this identification be true, it may be because of the power to embrace and to execute. The arms *hang*, when not *raised*. We shall not try to explain it any further here.

The man is shown hanging in a sling on one foot. Astrology teaches that the feet are ruled by the sign Pisces. The crossing of the legs is a symbol of ' crossing ' in general.

Among the other cards of the Greater Arcana, nine of which symbolise planetary principles and functions, three only are given in full as heavenly bodies: Sun, Moon and the—(eight-pointed)— 'Flaming Star,' while the significance of the others is clothed in allegorical images.

Now the question why only these three and not the other planetary principles should have been given in full, is difficult to answer. In a way the 'Flaming Star' stands for the stars in general and so this trinity means: Sun, Moon and Stars. On the other hand, ancient priests and astrologer-initiates appear not to have chosen to communicate more of the significance of the planets than just a few of their apparent effects, while in 'Sun, Moon and Star' they strongly expressed the idea of a Heavenly Trinity, viz. that of the positive or masculine creative power, radiating life; that of a feminine or negative power, which rules formation, and of a uniting principle, be it under the name of Law, Love or Union. The latter was always represented as specifically benefic. It is evidently the idea of the planet Venus, the beautiful morning and evening star, which was known to, and adored by, all peoples in all ages.

This trinity contains more meaning than a superficial astrological consideration could reveal. From such a standpoint it might even appear more or less arbitrary. So, for instance, the question might be asked, Why has not Mercury, nearer to the Sun even than Venus, been chosen as a member of the trinity? It would take us too far from our main road if we tried to explain this in detail, but it may be stated that in some respect the Moon represents and conveys the vibrations of Mercury to the Earth. The astrological symbols for the visible sun and for the planet we know under the name of Mercury, but which could as well have been named Vulcan, should be ♄ and ☊ respectively instead of ☉ and ☿. I have explained this in another volume. (*Cosmology* II, *Elements of Astrology*.) Further we might point out, that to the Earth and its inhabitants, the Sun, the Moon and Venus are, in fact, of some sort of *primary* importance ; the Sun and the Moon (of the Earth) as the representatives to us of the primary polar powers of the positive and the negative in Cosmos ; Venus as the planet representing the first step in evolution next to the Earth, consequently of primary importance to our evolution.

The Sun, Moon and ' Flaming Star ' are not only one of the most striking and beautiful expressions of the Divine Trinity among our present-day Free-masons, as every handbook on Freemasonry shows us, but have been so for long ages. A specimen of it is to be found on a couple of border-stones or steles, put along the frontier of his territory by the Chaldean king Melichikou (1144–1130 B.C.).* The heads of these steles bear a representation of the king and his daughter before a goddess (of Justice ?), and above these figures are the images of the Sun, the Moon and the (eight-pointed) Flaming Star, which evidently mean, that the king, eventually for the benefit of his daughter as well, invokes the Heavenly Powers of the Trinity to protect his kingdom against invasion. Another borderstone with the same figures of Sun, Moon and eight-pointed Flaming Star, even dates as far back as the year 1380 B.C., under the reign of King Nazi-Maraddach. So three thousand years ago the three Heavenly Lights appear to have been

* Musée du Louvre, Paris.

bearing the same significance and to have been used in this same mutual relation as at present in Freemasonry and in our Tarot system. We may accept this as pretty sure proof of the antiquity of both Freemasonry and Tarot.

XIII. *Death. Saturn.*

The picture speaks for itself—as indeed most of them do—but still there is more in it than we might suppose at first sight. Beyond all doubt it is a sort of allegorical representation of Father Chronos, Time, who, while creating, consumes his own children, and was very often pictured as a warning of death or a remembrance of mortality. But on the other hand Time marks the beginning, and birth is not less under his government than death. The ancient edition of this card shows the figure harvesting heads and limbs of human bodies upon a field. This may be an expression of an old superstition, which said that those limbs with which man sinned would grow out of his grave. Probably a distorted teaching of the Law of Karma or cosmic reaction, which is also ruled by Saturn, at least in the execution. And in this function he is the old God of Israel, whose law was "an eye for an eye and a tooth for a tooth."

But Saturn is more. He is the planet or cosmic function (let us say planet for convenience sake) of Formation, which means also determination in Place and Time, limitation, definition, etc.

Now let us see what *P.* says. He identifies the card with the principle of the Hebrew letter *Mem*, who "is a woman, the companion of man," and therefore gives rise to ideas of fertility, formation.

" It is pre-eminently the material and female, the local and plastic sign, an image of external and passive action." It is really a great pity, that this occultist never realised what he was saying, astrologically or cosmically. " *Mem* is one of the three mother-letters."

Saturn is the ruler of the Tenth house, Capricorn, which as such is called the house of the ' married woman ' in Hindu astrology.

That Saturn, the Christian Satan, has close relations with woman and even that he used her as his favourite vehicle or agent, is one of the Christian ' teachings,' in which we recognise distorted or perverted occult knowledge.

Death certainly is only relative and the death of the form may mean the commencement of life on another plane. Birth down here may be seen as a sort of death of a higher existence. " The veil and mask of life is perpetuated in change, transformation and passage from lower to higher . . ." (*W.*) Higher to lower as well. *W.* shows the figure on horseback, which is not inadequate for the ruler of Capricorn, which succeeds to Sagittarius : action and definition in space and time are born from thought. " . . . perpetual rebirth of the Being in the domain of Time." (*P.*)

XIV. *Temperance. Mercury.*

" . . . the Genius of the Sun holding two cups and pouring from the one into the other the liquor which holds life." (*P.*)—" A winged angel with the sign of the sun upon his forehead . . . pouring the essences of life from chalice to chalice." (*W.*) Another version has : " . . . pours the fluid of Life from a golden vase into a silver one." (P.) This is evidently the cosmic function next to the Sun, messenger of the same : Mercury or Vulcan, lord of the sphere of Virgo, surrounding the solar Leo-sphere. Other traditional descriptions confirm this : " It is the symbol of combinations, working incessantly in all regions of Nature." (P.) On his breast this angel bears a square with inscribed triangle, reminding us of the passage of the cosmological *Stanzas of Dzyan*, " The Three fall into the Four," which means the beginning of Manifestation. " Entry of Spirit into Matter and reaction of Matter upon Spirit." (P.) So on the subject of this card there seems to be perfect understanding. " Incarnation of Life," P. adds. This is Mercury, who has to do with the distribution of life-currents from the Sun farther on into the solar-system and from the heart and solar-plexus farther on into our physical body. The golden vase and the silver one illustrate this distribution from higher to lower regions.

So this card signifies all sorts of distribution, from the nervous system and its workings of co-ordination to correspondence by the post office, letters and communications, and the latter not only limited to this physical world but extended to other planes of existence. The function of Mercury is that of the mind in its concrete activities and imparts knowledge, learning, which after all is the beginning or potentiality of all our further relations in this world.

P. seeks to establish relation between it and the Hebrew letter *Nun*, which means " the offspring of the female—(we said rightly, that Mercury has much to do with the Moon)—a son, the fruit of any kind . . . the image of the being produced or reflected. . . "

Yes : reflection and above all reproduction. The name 'Temperance' appears to have been chosen because of the transposition from one plane to another, or one centre to another, which has much to do with 'time' also. The latter is the proper reason for naming this principle directly after that of Saturn.

XV. *The Devil. Mars.*

The goat-like figure recalls the sign Capricorn in which astrology teaches that the planet Mars has its exaltation, the name 'devil' means the evil, as is well known, and this alliteration holds good not only in English. It is the symbol of that which to exoteric human understanding is as much of a malefic nature as Venus is benefic. The counterpart of Venus : Mars, planet of pain and struggle, passion and sex-nature, but also of the energy necessary for the process of formation and generation in Nature. Allusion to sex-problems is found in the two human figures, man and woman, chained to the pedestal on which the diabolic figure is seated. That sex-nature binds man, is a natural fact of a more or less occult order.

So it has to do with generation in Nature in every sense and kingdom, though astrology teaches that Mars has a special connection with the animal kingdom and animal passion—passion which drives to the preservation of the body as well as of the race ; fighting for existence in both senses of the term. So Mars always figured as the War-lord. Not only sexual energy, but every energy in Nature chains the result to the cause and object to subject. It is unnecessary to work this out any further. We shall be safe in interpreting this card as energy, desire, lust, war, struggle, difficulties, pain, loss, etc. But also as exercise, training ; tests to which the personality will be subject.

The torch in the hand of the figure denotes, of course, the fire of passion and desire, which may rise to anger, etc. So it may well be said to represent the condition of " Adam and Eve after the Fall " (*W.*) The struggle for existence, in short.

P. in regard to this card points to the Hebrew letter " *Samech* which expresses the same hieroglyphic sign as the *Zain* (7th arcanum) . . . etc., a weapon of any kind . . . " We can see, that this generative force has much to do with the house of marriage.

XVI. *The Tower. Uranus.*

" Occult explanations attached to this card are meagre and mostly disconcerting." (*W.*) The reason for this is easily seen : the principles of Uranus and Neptune were not much known in antiquity save that they were the general principles of the Heavens (the Air or also the atmosphere) and the Ocean, and as such we find them in the Pantheon and in the original Tarot, not yet as the much later discovered planets, which personify these general cosmic principles. Later ages added very little, if anything at all, to those original explanations. Still Ouranos and Poseidon were known in Greece as well as Dourga and Varouna in India.

And the stone tower struck by a flash of lightning is another version of the legend of Ouranos mutilating his son Chronos, which means, that Heaven is not content with a body of fixed dimensions and form, nor any heavenly force with the limitations put to it by physical authorities or architects. This may warn man, not to build upon physical existence alone or to think himself safe upon a material basis, however high and solid it may appear from a material point of view. The general meaning, however, is not incidental but essential. ". . . the ruin of the house of life, when evil has prevailed therein " (*W.*) is one of many possible occurrences ; it may signify ' blighted ambitions and hopes,' etc. (*P.*), but the universal and every day significance is : the renewal of the form, or rather of embodied life, by the force of Heaven, and of microcosm by the life of macrocosm, which incidentally of course breaks up forms here and there, if they are no longer fit for survival ; the house of doctrine as well as every structure made by vanity, dogmatism and separativeness.

The Hebrew letter *Ayin* is addicted to this card. *P.* utterly fails in giving any elucidation of this relationship. *W.* has put it very clearly in this quotation : " Except the Lord build the house, they labour in vain that build it."

So the card of the Tower signifies the relation between macro- and micro-cosm and will mean rupture, sudden disillusion, disenchantment, but also it symbolises intuition, renewal, help from above and clear insight in relation to vanity and sham projects, illusion and meaningless formalism.

XVII. *The Star. Venus.*

" The figure expresses eternal youth and beauty." No astrologer will hesitate to recognise Venus. " The Star is the *étoile flamboyante*, which appears in Masonic symbolism, but has been confused herein." (*W.*) And " gifts of the spirit," which *au fond* means beauty, are the gifts administered by Venus, who in the solar system hands over the vibrations or ' gifts ' coming from the Sun, to our Earth. The picture on the card shows it quite clearly : a naked girl, demonstrating undoubtedly the beauty of the human body, symbol of beauty in the nature of man, pouring " the fluids of Life upon the Earth (and the sea : i.e. into soul and body—Th.) from two cups, the one of gold and the other of silver." (*P.*) " The genius of the Sun has now descended to Earth under the form of this young girl, the image of eternal Youth." (*P.*) Well, then it is the image of this planet of beauty and eternal youth, which has its place between the Sun and Mercury on one side and our Earth on the other, the third personification of the genius of the Sun.   The ibis and the butterfly connect the idea of immortality with this figure, in perfect accord with the mystic teaching which says, that love extends beyond the grave.

" The *Phe*—identified with this card—expresses the same hieroglyphic value as the *Beth* (second card), but in a more extended sense." It is said to represent speech. (*P.*) Now Venus has in so far to do with the second sign, that it rules this sign. The ' more extended sense ' may perhaps be thought of as this planetary rulership, as " the Word in action in Nature with all its consequences." (*P.*) Venus could perhaps be seen in the sense it has in the Gospel of St. John : " The Word which became the Light of men."   Venus indeed is the representative of the ruler of Light on Earth and in Nature : third aspect of the Solar Logos.

" The Word in action in Nature with all its consequences," we should like to correct in this way :

it is Venus, the ruler of the signs Taurus and Libra, houses of riches, art, beauty, and of the organised body. In the latter it represents the Law of Harmony between the Self and the Not-self.

In divination it means of course benefit, well-doing, organisation, co-operation, love, beauty, peace, concord, etc. The reverse of the card of Mars. As the contrary of energy it may mean laziness, indolence, rest, weakness.

XVIII. *The Moon.*

Everything that has been said in astrology about the Moon might be repeated here, as there exists no controversy whatever on the point of identity. " The card represents life of the imagination apart from life of the spirit." (*W.*)

This card consequently means the life of the soul in particular, the feelings and sentiments, emotions (not only fear, etc.), changes wrought in existence by them, water and the female element in general. In the horoscopic figure it may be the mother or some other woman prominent in the life of the querent; it may signify women in general (and morally or psychically, while Saturn means physical woman). It is the sign of *panta rei* : everything passing, flowing or ebbing away in life, consequently uncertainty. It may relate to dreams, to exhibitions, popular plays, and games, theatres, and to the lower class of people. Physically it means the brain and the stomach.

The hieroglyphic value of the Hebrew letter *Tzaddi*, connected with this card, " is the same as that of *Thet* (ninth card) . . . which perhaps may account for the relationship of the Moon with that house, as pointed out by us before. It should mean a term, an aim, an end." (*P.*) But this does not make it much clearer.

P. has only one good thing on it, and after all this is only on a particular and not very high level : " Servile spirits (the dog), savage souls (the wolf), and crawling creatures (the crayfish) are all present watching the fall of the soul, hoping to aid in its destruction." That is true. And it may happen to us, that a lower current of the Moon brings our way people who have no higher aim than to ' aid in our destruction ' even if we ourselves have no intention whatever of ' falling '.

XIX. *The Sun.*

" The walls indicate, that we are still in the visible, or material world." (*P.*) This relates to the picture which shows a child on horseback—or two children as in the older editions of the card—playing beneath the bright Sun and evidently within a walled enclosure. So far so good : we are and we remain in this world. And for the rest the Sun is the Sun and this card means everything that astrology can tell about the Sun, in every respect and on all planes. It means the positive or masculine elements in general, the power and function of will and concentration, great benefit and mighty protection in spiritual as well as in mundane life and matters. It may signify the father of the querent and high authorities, king, president, ruler, etc. The spiritual centre of man and the centre of importance in everything is indicated by it. Physically it indicates the heart and the solar-plexus.

The protecting power of the Sun is well illustrated

by " the hieroglyphic value of the Hebrew letter *Quoph,* which expresses a sharp weapon, everything that is useful to man, that defends him and makes an effort for him." (*P.*).

In a figure laid for divination this card indicates the centre of interest and that which is fixed, certain, assured and under protection.

XX. *The Last Judgment. Jupiter.*

If Saturn denotes ' death ' and the grave, what more natural than that his counterpart Jupiter should stand for the resurrection from the grave ? While Saturn, Lord of the mineral kingdom, is held to ' kill ' by his crystallising effect, Jupiter, Lord of the vegetable kingdom and of all that grows and expands and evolves, leading up to sublimation and elevation, abstraction, etc., afterwards, is first the emblem and function of *organic life,* later on also those of psychic and spiritual life above the material existence, barren and naked, from which it consequently brings deliverance. The latter meaning is chiefly viewed when symbolising this principle in the card of the Last Judgment. " An angel sounds his trumpet *per sepulchra regionum* and the dead arise." (*W.*) Some people say " that it signifies renewal, which is obvious enough . . ." and " that it is the generative force of the earth and eternal life." (*W.*) The latter fairly covers our definition of Jupiter's function. Again *W.* further mentions, that it " is the card which registers the accomplishment of the great work of transformation." Which is also in the line of Jupiter, *Io Pater,* ' Our Father that is in the Heavens.' And every great work needs his co-operation ; there is no important or great work done in this world without Jupiter, the planet of ideals playing a prominent rôle in it. Ideals, that " are the angel part of us," as *Zanoni* tells his disciple. So this card stands for ideals, religious, social or any other and for the elevating effect they have on man ; for ideas and leading motives, aspirations, etc., consequently for generalisation, illumination, dispersion, elevation, for all that is honourable on one hand but also for illusions or vain aspirations on the other hand. It is the sign of deliverance from narrow thought and hampering conditions in the soul as well as in the body and in life.

The card is identified with the Hebrew letter *Resh*, which " is the head of man, and it is therefore associated with the idea of all that possesses in itself an original, determined movement. It is the absolute sign of motion, good or bad, and expresses the renewal of things with regard to their innate power of motion."—" Return to the divine world."—" Vegetable life." (*P*.) Yes. We might say : thought-power and the idea of motion which it implies and imparts. Jupiter was the first and chief of the Gods, *Theoi*, Movers.

XXI. *The World. Neptune.*

As in the case of Uranus we want to point out that originally the planet cannot have been appointed, astronomically, but the principle of cosmic magetism, of which it is the organ, and the universal magnetised, field, the field of the world in which we live, must have been well known to the initiates, who worshipped Poseidon and Varuna, gods of the world-ocean. The symbols of the four fixed signs are presented at the corners of the cards, and where these fixed signs are seen as the foundation stones of our physical world by such visionaries as Ezechiel and St. John of Patmos, we cannot be far wrong in assuming that originally the meaning was that of the physical world coming forth out of the magnetised etheric ocean of the universe, which itself has been represented by the *oval* form, be it a laurel wreath or something else. The World must have had a larger meaning, originally, than that of the world of beings moving on the surface of our Earth, and the oval figure may well have stood for the form of the solar system at large, with its planets moving in oval orbs.

Appropriated to the world of men, it must mean that which falls outside our will-power, cosmic conditions to which we are subject, but which at the same time provide us with all that is wanted for our physical conditions. The latter of course became the reason for attaching to this card a generally benefic influence, especially in the domain of the senses. " It is eloquent as an image of the swirl of the sensitive life, of joy attained in the body, of the soul's intoxication—(can any word remind us more strongly of Neptune's workings than precisely this one : ' intoxication ' ?—Th.)—in the earthly paradise, but still guarded by the Divine Watchers . . ." (*W*.) Let us put it this way : it means that if we row with the cosmic tide, we shall enjoy happiness and everything we want, but on the other hand we must not neglect the implicit possibility, that when rowing against the tidal current of the world, we shall experience trouble and no end of it, or if we ' cross the stream ' we shall have to stand firm on our legs. So besides the joy of the senses, this card means also the cosmic origin of life, to which the candidate for initiation returns, and which now and then appears in dreams. In fact this card has much to do with dream-life. The relations of Neptune with the Moon and the lunar body are not unknown to astrologers nowadays.

The Hebrew letter *Tau* is related to this card and " has the same hieroglyphic meaning as the *Daleth* (fourth card)—that is the womb ;—(which confirms the relationship to the Moon—Th.)—but it is chiefly the sign of reciprocity, the image of all that is mutual, reciprocal." It is further added that abundance and perfection lie in the card. (*P.*) Reciprocal certainly : from that we come and to that we shall return, be it the world's dust or the ether of the cosmic ocean.

Very striking is *P.'s* saying that " This symbol represents macrocosm and microcosm . . ." and even more so that " the empire of the world belongs to the empire of Light, and the empire of Light is the throne of God . . ." Scientifically expressed : the ethereal world, being the bearer of light, is the universal womb of the material or physical world. The nude female figure may certainly contain indications with regard to the life of the senses, but is also a symbol of the angelic state to which man will one day come after being delivered from the bonds of the lower world. It may have to do with nature spirits. It is Aphrodite rising from the sea, daughter of Neptune. Beauty and love and happiness arising from the communion of souls.

O. (Zero) *The Fool. Our Earth.*

The average stage of man in the present stage of Earth-evolution is ' human,' but not yet at the stage

F

of wisdom, consequently that of the ' unwise man.'
To us, creatures living upon the Earth, this globe
cannot be observed by us *in toto,* and the Fool is
represented as a man walking without paying attention to himself. There is something of absolute Fate
about this figure, which reminds us of the old saying
of astrologers : " The wise man rules his stars, the
fool obeys them." On the point of this fatality all
authorities agree. For the rest the explanation does
not seem very satisfying. To us there appears to
be no doubt regarding the nature of this Fool, presented as a final ' principle,' if we may call it that,
after those of the planets. A principle, however,
without a number, a principle of nothing, nothing-
ness.

The planets give us the symbols or ideas of organs
of consciousness, the zodiacal signs denote modes
of substance, from which consciousness is derived.
So the *zero*-principle is the symbol of *un*consciousness. In fact he who is unconscious, of himself or of
Self, will obey every intimation from without and
obeys ' his stars '—his senses, stupidly, blindly.

Of course this card has much to do with foolishness, spiritual dumbness, but it bears also the meaning of that which cannot be helped and which we
do best to leave altogether aside ; or that which will
come right of itself and need not be heeded by us :
that to which we are subject, as to the Earth course
in its orbit. It does not need our personal assistance.
Realising the latter fact this ' fool ' might after all
appear to be wiser than a good many other people,
who in their human vanity imagine they are greatly
needed for carrying out the intentions of their God,
of Whom they claim a sort of personal knowledge.

A proverb says, that children and fools tell the truth. Taken as a whole, the card signifies that which will prove to contain more truth than appears ; that which cannot be helped ; those who are unconscious (of certain things, e.g.,) or unreasonable or foolish, disregarding logical propositions and actions. Also that part of our surroundings over which we have no control or which we do not master ; that which we have to obey or which we ignore.

The Hebrew letter *Shin* is brought in relation with this card, and *P.* says it means " the Motion of relative duration," but his explanation does not throw any particular light on the card nor on the relationship. The picture seems to hint also that the fool " is hurried to his destruction unawares." (*W.*) And there may be a good deal in it. In divination it may hint at persons suffering under this tendency.

The question may be asked, why the planetary cards have been named in this order. When we agree that Mercury, Temperance, has been put in the place of Jupiter, which after all has been used in a higher octave, we see first named the three planets outside the place of the Earth, governing the building of the physical mould and having to do with the birth and death of it. Then follows the planet of cosmic electricity and of the birth of human spirit in the physical building, which it eventually destroys. Next come the three planetary principles functioning on the spiritual side, which have their meaning only after the birth of human spirit. The Moon takes the place of Mercury-Vulcan, and the order is that of reckoning from the Earth, consequently in a continuous line from the outside :

Venus—Moon (for Mercury-Vulcan)—Sun. They have to do with the growth of body and soul. Finally the principle of deliverance from the prison of the body : Jupiter, and that of the cosmic ocean to which the particles return, Universal solvent ; ocean which constitutes the real ground for our practical unity in the world. The Fool as the denial of all sense, nonsense.

There may be other explanations of course. The one offered here seems to have the advantage that it is in the line of the suggestion, made before, viz. that the whole system of the Tarot is a sort of symbolism, expressly adapting cosmic principles to human life and to man's personal interests, not always even in the highest sense.

There exists a remarkable difference between the degree of clearness with which concrete particulars of the Lesser Arcana are given, and the diffuse teaching of the Greater Arcana, which appears to have been rather covered and veiled, than divulged. It was in the first place the Lesser Arcana, with which the *diseurs de bonne aventure* wanted to please their clients, so it naturally had their chief attention.

It is still more remarkable that all explanation about the ' why ' of the Lesser Arcana fails. We ought perhaps to take into account a meagre effort made by Papus in his *Tarot of the Bohemians*, (p. 235–237), where he tries to assign each of the cards to one of the decanates of the zodiac ; but he makes no further use of the hypothesis. For the rest I venture to say that it does not hold good at all and does not in the least correspond with the traditional significances given, as the authors tell us, in respect of the

Bohemians. Another equally unsuccessful effort at explanation has been made recently by a pupil of Eteilla, d'Odoucet and Papus, a Frenchman calling himself Ely Alta, in a book entitled *Le Tarot Egyptien* (1922), which bears a close resemblance to that of Papus or speaks of the very same source as the latter. In fact Alta reproduces a treatise of Eteilla's disciple and co-worker d'Odoucet and gives more than Papus in so far as he preludes every significance of a card in the Lesser Arcana with a sort of explanation in a would-be cosmogonical sense. The fact is, that these explanations all fall short of explaining the traditional significance. So they cannot be more than a sort of drapery of eloquence, hung over the tableaux by later commentators, perhaps by Eteilla himself. And the only thing they divulge without any doubt at all is that the key to these 'lesser' mysteries has been lost or has never been given out to those to whom this practice of divination has been presented " as a bible which would make their living at the same time," as Papus has said somewhere.

But the striking fact is, that these traditional significations cover almost exactly and in almost every card the theory expounded by us. So we may be fairly certain that this theory contains or *is* the very key. We shall verify it systematically and card for card.

THE LESSER ARCANA

The theory formulated in the first part of the present work must be proved by practice ; and here we are in the same lucky position as with horoscopy, where we find also the most abstract world-vision combined with the natural facts of everyday life : religion, philosophy and science in one and testified to by facts, which can be verified by every serious student, as easily as the facts of any other branch of natural science.

We shall now deal with the Arcana Minor much on the same lines as we have followed with the cards of the Arcana Major, only still more abridged, if possible, in order to make the work clear and the supervision easy, and so produce a handbook, as simple and practical as possible for use in the practice of divination. We shall therefore first give the generally accepted traditional meanings of each card, and then derive the significance from the given theory.

The qualifications which we think fully justified by the theory, will be put in italics.

We use as illustrations the pictures of the cards as they have been drawn on the authority of Mr. A. E. Waite and published by Messrs. Rider and Co., Paternoster Row, London.

Practical divination speaks of two ways in which the cards, in general, have to be or can be interpreted : *right* and *reversed*, and the professors of the art say it depends on the way the cards fall when they are laid after being shuffled ; it may be the image of the card comes ' right,' i.e. facing the querent, or upside down. The latter is called ' reversed.' This appears to me to be a rather arbitrary distinction, because of course it costs you no trouble to put all cards ' right ' before shuffling and to keep them right all the time. But there may be actually a stronger and a weaker side to each card of the Lesser Arcana, as it may act on the higher or on the lower side of human nature, or it may stand for ourselves or for our opponents ; it may either be fortified by benefic influences of neighbouring cards and the planets, or weakened by malefics. So we shall not protest against the term ' reversed,' but use it in a different way and consider it simply as the pathological side of the genuine significance, if we may be allowed to express it thus. Nor shall we indicate it separately, but simply leave it to the consideration of the professor of divination to decide if a fall is weak or more or less pathological.

We might add one more remark, viz. regarding the nature of the Page and the Knight. We place the Knight after the Page, which makes the former fall upon the houses of Water and the Page on the houses of Air. Tradition gives first the Knight and after him the Page. Astrologers will feel the essential difference between both : the one is of the nature of Air, the other of the nature of Water. The latter is more ' essential,' working on the sentiments, while the Page is rather working on the intellectual plane of existence. The Knight brings the inner change and link, the Page the outer change and connection. Of the two the Page or Knave is the lesser or younger. Evidently the symbolic figures have been chosen so as to express a difference of this kind. The page may become a knight, after he has won experience. Now ' experience ' is the typical function of the houses or signs of *Water*. The page-period in mediæval society was that of the disciple, of assisting, learning ; of carrying messages : all this is typical of houses or signs of Air. The name of *Knave*, sometimes substituted for Page, is doubtlessly given to indicate the ' secondary ' importance of " those people " in relation to the nobility of the other.

Air-people are always more or less 'profane' in relation to water-people, and this has been evidently expressed in the mediæval denomination.

WANDS

Ace

TRADITION : Birth, source, principle, beginning, origin, cause, reason, creation, invention. Some say also : family, but this is probably to be taken as 'family-descent,' or parentage or origin of the family, which is a different idea. Reversed : Fall, perdition, decadence, decline, ruin, etc.

THEORY : The element of *Air* on the *First house* or ascendant has of course to do with birth and beginning, because it is the coming through of the message from above to the regions of the physical plane ; the ascendant indeed is the synthesised appearance of the heavens at the beginning of . . . whatever it may be, and so this card signifies on one hand the inflow of light from above into the world of matter and fact, which can have several meanings. On the other hand, seen from the side of light itself, it is the 'fall in matter' and the decline of the higher, as well as the enlightening of the lower. The cards of the airy element have always and in every instance a double meaning and not only in the sense of right and reversed, but a meaning on two sides. And apparently this has been wrongly introduced as 'right' or 'reversed' in some cases. So the ace of wands will represent the effect of suddenness, of the incidental, even accidental, showing some appearances of the planet Uranus. It denotes something that is making its appearance all of a sudden ; a sort of manifestation, creation such as the birth of a child. This, by the way, is generally considered to be a joy for the parents, etc., but may not be for the soul, which has to accept once more the limitations of life in a body of earth. And this is the two-sidedness of the significance.

CONCLUSION : *Birth, beginning, innovation, creation' initiative, impulse, origin, principle, source, cause' reason, parentage, handing over of a message, news' revelation, initiation.* On the other hand come the meanings derived from *fall, decline, descent, depreciation, profanation, etc.* But it means *that which will happen once only* and which cannot be taken back.

Two

TRADITION : Melancholy, sadness, surprise, as tonishment, consternation, terror, fear, enchantment, trouble, but also on the other hand riches, fortune and magnificence.

THEORY : *Air* on the *Second house,* that of Taurus, which explains at once the latter significances ascribed to the card by some authors ; the other category of definitions derives from the earthy nature of the Second house, which, put into the tone of the airy element, may cause something of the oppression, which the heaviness of this fixed and earthy house exercises on the mind. It is the impression of heaviness, of a load on the back, which easily may attain the more concise form of a fear, a gloom, a feeling of being downcast, impotent, weak and not able to resist circumstances. So it may signify the pressure of material conditions, the responsibility imparted by riches, but also projects or conceptions of an economical nature and the idea of capital and capitalising. Further the combination of the principles of air with the house of Taurus must give music, and we may be sure that this card always has some significance in that way and in the sphere of art intellectually and in general. This is a very important significance.

CONCLUSION : *Music, art, artistic ability in general ; capital, riches, heavy responsibility, pressure, obsession, melancholy, fear, weakness, impossibility or material power (on one side and on the other), gloom, dullness, ' spleen,' impotence, subjection to material circumstances ; attitude of ' wait and see ' ; the future is for those that can (afford to) wait. Country life.*

Three

TRADITION : Enterprise, effort, essay, trade, commerce, discovery, usurpation, daring, temerity and also imprudence, interruption, cessation and ' the end of troubles,' discontinuative.

THEORY : The rather contradictory descriptions of this card's significance are well explained by its zodiacal position : *Air* on the *Third house*, which doubles the influence of ' air ' and of the mercurial vibrations and effects. This card has the accent of the suit of wands. It must consequently denote : communication, reflection and all that comes from these. This needs little explanation.

CONCLUSION : *Communication, instruction, reflexion, message, writing, postage and letters, superficial know-*

ledge, airiness, passing impressions, discontinuance, interruption, change, perhaps a certain amount of *geniality, imprudence* also ; neglect or want of proper attention ; as to ' temerity ' I should say only in so far as this means an *easy manner of overcoming obstacles, quick insight ; effort, essay, trade* are correct. Mercury being the God of merchants, and thieves, this card may relate to *commerce, theft and loss.* " *The end of troubles* " is indeed well said, because this card gives the key for their solution and shows the way of escape.

Four

TRADITION : Society, association, alliance, multitude and all that implies a gathering of men, even armies ; mixture ; country life, felicity, augmentation, prosperity, happiness, peace and concord, etc., convocation ; advance.

THEORY : It is *Air* on the *Fourth house* and the mixing of mercurial and lunar influence will of course explain the idea of gathering. We cannot quite see some of the definitions (contract, pact, treaty), but generally we find the idea of that which binds together by memory and common motives, thoughts, mottos common to a certain group of people, be it family or nation, clan or army. So this leads us to see in the card the expression of the common motive, of that which binds people together. It is not the contract, but the motive which afterwards leads to contracts, or from which the contract will result. A common mistake, in astrological descriptions as well, is this mixing up of definitions relating to the cause and to the effect respectively. Mercury brooding over the house of the family and the moon, engenders homely feelings, memories, thoughts of internal service, household matters, and tends more or less to a profane and familiar or descriptive language, to joke, fun and the theatrical art, to inviting people to come together and have their share in weal and woe. It represents also common sense, which, however, remains in many cases ' common ' enough. And it contains the motives, which actually govern the facts and actions in this world.

CONCLUSION : *Family-spirit, clan, home, the ideas and motives which rule us,* consequently *that which is familiar to us ; memory, reminiscences, brooding and scheming, fantasy, theatrical arts, fancy, imagination.* It can be *augmentation* as well as *decrease,* it generally means *change and unstable conditions, popularity and vaccillation, profanation.* It may denote some *group of people, a gathering or meeting, family-council. A convocation. a call and a vote. Cosiness.*

Five

TRADITION : Gold, riches, opulence, magnificence, brilliancy, luxury, the struggle for riches, " physical, philosophical and moral sun." (P.) But also process, trickery, contradiction, discussion, chicane, etc.

THEORY : *Air* on the *Fifth house* : that of the sun. The house of the heart and of children, of speculation and love affairs, of pride and of will-power. There is more of the richness of the heart in it than of material abundance, though generally Leo-people know how to reach the latter. It is a house of Fire, and the combination of Fire and Air makes warm air, which may be used to heat rooms, in the same way as words, that contain warm feelings of the heart, will do good to other people, and on the other hand hot speech will arouse lively contradiction. Here is the same mistake : the card is not that of contradiction, but of hot speech, very positive expression, and contentions, suggestions, rather than discussion, egocentric thought, from which we may conclude, that it will evoke contradiction, or some other effect. But we have to do with the proper meaning of a card itself. It is quite true, that the house Leo may bring gold and presents. Thought-power taken to heart, or taking its motives from love and from the desires and wishes of the heart, may very often be more selfish than reasonable, but it is a real pushing power and therefore generally is the most helpful element towards attaining the goal. This, of course, has been the reason for ascribing riches, etc., to this card.

CONCLUSION : *Egotism, positive speech, contention, persuasion, suggestion, hot speech, demonstration (e.g. of love or desire) ; pushing power ;* all this may lead to *trickery,* to *competition* perhaps, and to *struggle for riches* certainly ; it means *speaking and thinking in such a self-centred way, that no notice is taken of other people's standpoint ;* consequently *clashing of opinions ;* sometimes it may allude to *gold and presents, but to the promise rather than to the fact.* There is *little or no evil* in this card. At most it may denote *stupid and childish persistence in one's own personal opinion, e.g. wishes.* It has something *sunny* in it and is *good for health and wealth in a general way,* promoting both, but it *is not* ' riches ' in itself.

Six

TRADITION : Servant, inferior, mercenary man, commissioner ; interior of a house, the household ; it is also said to denote great news and expectation, hope and trust, but sometimes not without some misgivings or a slight apprehension of treachery.

THEORY : It is *Air* on the house of Virgo, the *Sixth*, house of the servants and work, of exact science and the academy, of health and food, of the art of decoration and the interior of the house, as well as of the retail dealer. The element of thought (Air) on the earthy house of Virgo must naturally bring forth knowledge of every detail and reveal mistakes or shortcomings ; it promotes efficiency, and the latter is one of the principal meanings of the card. Here again is a double mercurial expression, so this card must denote special abilities, capacities, technical insight ; moreover food questions and medicine, medicaments and nursing ; practical arrangement of details, but as Virgo " kills the prophets," this card may contain some or other discrepancy in the philosophical or logical, theoretical or strictly just side of things.

CONCLUSION : *Knowledge, exact and academical, decorative art, efficiency, work, servitude and servants, practical solution of problems, but at the same time perhaps some discrepancy ; food, medicine, treatment, experiment ;* it may relate to *persons in every subordinate position and to retail tradesmen ;* the personal attitude under this card is rather passive and indeed that of *expectation, attention, waiting for orders or for the result of experiments, for the answer on question or demand ; solicitation.*

Seven

TRADITION : Discussion, negotiation, conference, conversation, deliberation, dissertation ; measure ; correspondence, words and language ; generally success, but there may be also some hesitation, uncertainty, irresolution, light-heartedness.

THEORY : All this is very strikingly typifying the element *Air* on the *Seventh house*, that of the airy Libra, house of relationship, marriage, meeting of the Self and the Not-self, which rules contracts, books and manuscripts. Here only comes ' discussion ' into play. In the Fifth house the individuality was alone, and for discussion you want two persons.

CONCLUSION : *Discussion, relation, negotiation, entertainment, discourse, lecture, reasonable explanation, contract, marriage proposed, society-rulership and orders given out to inferiors, arrangements, regularisation and measurement ; measure, proportion, rules given for conduct.* There is *uncertainty or opportunism* in so far as rules are given in relation to circumstances, which may change. The personal interests are brought in, in relation with those of others. *Fair weather.*

Eight

TRADITION : Examination, interior disputes, misunderstanding, regrets, interior agitation, scruples, doubt, repentance, etc. But on the other hand it is brought into connection with everything that has to do with country life, the fields, gardens, woods, etc. Also : pleasure, amusement, enjoyment, recreation. Quite apart from all this : an express messenger, the arrows of love or the arrows of jealousy. " Great haste, great hope, speed towards an end, which promises assured felicity." (*W*.)

THEORY : The card represents *Air* on the *Eighth house* and the influence of Scorpio will make the mind acute and sharp, so as to investigate and to examine the most hidden riddles, while in this house the mind comes to the sensation or consciousness of pleasure and pain, thirst and drinking. (The chalice will begin its suit later on the Ninth house.) It is the house of hidden and 'forbidden' knowledge or rather experience. The 'arrows of love' actually mean passion, and the 'arrows of jealousy,' the common counterpart of the same. The sensation of sex is born in this house and indicated by this card. As to swift or speedy messages, this may sometimes happen, because the Scorpion is sometimes very sudden in its movements. What the card should have to do with country life is less evident. We should say rather that it must stand in relation with the sea, fishermen and sailors. The mind in this house is very critical and sharp-witted, sometimes subject to doubt and misgivings, superstition and jealousy. It is in search of truth and enjoyment. Artistic abilities will run along the line of poetry, music and sculpture. It has always to do with the hidden side of things, the interior, or the inner life.

CONCLUSION : *Examination, interrogation, internal or inner conceptions, knowledge and disputes ; misgivings, doubt and sometimes misunderstandings ; quick response, reaction, and answer to unspoken words or meanings. The sensation of pleasure and pain, but at*

*the same time the knowledge and the occasion to avoid
both or to get the one and avoid the other. Life at or
on the sea ; sailors and fishermen. Searchers for the
hidden side of things, students of occultism. Poetry,
music and sculpture. Secret message ; hidden meaning ;
sex questions. Private interview or rendez-vous. Bad
weather.*

Nine

TRADITION : Obstacle, delay, suspense, adversity,
slowness, contrariety, calamity, misfortune, renvoy,
trouble.

" The card signifies strength in opposition. If
attacked he will meet the onslaught boldly." (*W.*)

THEORY : The element of *Air* on the *Ninth house*,
which is opposite to that in which the particular
accent of the suit of wands lies : Gemini, the third.
This opposition evidently has been the chief motive
for the qualifications given in respect of this card in
the past.

There is a good deal in it, but not everything. Of
course, if the third house is the typical expression
of the ' message,' the Sagittarian is the type of the
man " who is always in the opposition," but he is
more. He is also . . . himself. This card seems
to be queerly veiled. It is at least strange to find
only malific expressions of the co-ordination of the
element Air and the principle of mind with the
house of Sagittarius, the thinker. This looks as if
the patrons of the Tarot system did not think it wise
to tell much about this sign of the prophets to the
fortune-telling gypsies. How this may be does not
concern us any further. Evidently the card must

G

have to do with prophecy, fortune-telling, teaching, conducting, guiding and the persons of guides, teachers, masters ; it must give the notion of travelling and far-reaching schemes, the faculty of speaking foreign languages and of writing, but it is true, that the persons indicated by this card find their "strength in opposition"—as W. has it—and very often therefore are in search of some convenient opponent or opposing force. It means intellectual chasing, sport, hunting, journalism and the raising of spirits, that are not easily to be got rid of afterwards. The latter fact accounts for all that has been said about obstacles, etc.

CONCLUSION : *Teaching, instruction, guidance, teachers, masters, guides. Planning, travelling, sport ; journalism, editors and journalists, public lecturers, orators ; prophecy and predicting.* On the other hand there may be unruliness, waywardness and unpractical idealism. It is certain that, where this card appears, much *controversy, contradiction, antagonism, mental strife,* etc., will be aroused, sometimes more than would appear necessary. There is also in it *extension of thought, spreading of news, rumours, preaching, excitement of the people and revolution.*

Ten

TRADITION : Treachery, duplicity, perfidy, falsehood, disguise, imposture, conspiration, obstacle, surprise, dissimulation, contrarieties, difficulties, falseseeming, oppression. " . . . and if there is question of a lawsuit, there will be certain loss." (*W.*)

THEORY : *Air* on the house of Capricorn : the *Tenth.* It is well known by astrologers, that the tenth house rules the actions, deeds and attitude. Also the name and official position of the personality in the world and at the same time the superiors or authorities, met with on account of position and activities. Actions and deeds, under the influence of the double-natured mercurial element, may easily degrade into ' double-dealing ' and everything else of that nature. But once more it appears to us, that the gypsy tradition is rather too much exclusively on the lower side of things. The qualities mixed here make very often an egoistic blend and a nature which reveals several weaknesses, as soon as it comes under trial. So the card on the one hand means certainly that the attitude of mind or action will be untrustworthy and must not be relied upon. There is fear and cowardice in it. But on the other hand the combination is that of mental ability, quick perception, etc. It means also the load of the earthy responsibility laid upon the shoulders of an airy creature, consequently ' oppression ' is a word very much to the point here. And this explains even why weaker natures are driven to undesirable, unreliable actions and reactions by it ; they cannot stand the pressure. Strong natures, however, accept the pressure as natural necessity, *karma*, and carry their burden. This is symbolised by the man carrying the ten wands. It is a symbol of executive ability, production, the doing of necessary things, obedience to official order and rule ; officials, ' red tape ' and burdens that appear heavier than they actually are.

CONCLUSION : *Karma, obedience, executive ability, production and reproduction, necessity ; officials and official position.* In weaker cases : *Duplicity, false-*

hood, unreliability, disguise, double-dealing, false appearance, lies and false diplomacy, etc. Oppression and overestimating the importance of things.

King

TRADITION : Country gentleman, man with good intentions and yet severe, honest and conscientious ; may be a peasant or agriculturist. Eteilla calls him the father. Marriage, union.

THEORY : Higher octave of the ace, lord of the suit of *Air* and the mind ; coming on the *First house.* What may have led to the legend of calling him a country gentleman and bringing the whole suit of wands more or less in relation with the country, is not clear. He is the lord of the intellectual kingdom, consequently he may denote every authority or personality of primary importance in some or other intellectual, mercurial or mercenary line. It must be some one representing a high authority himself or uniting opposite interests, while he himself, on account of the same authority he represents, may not or cannot be contradicted.

Now we want to put in a remark here concerning the court or personal cards in general : in the practice of divination they are generally taken to indicate persons, and this comes out very often right enough. Still they ought first to be considered as principles ; the personification of these principles in men and women comes in the second place only, but is important, of course, in our daily life. So the King of Wands must represent intellectual authority, mastership in the domain of the mind, trade and language.

CONCLUSION : *A governor, director of business, high official, postmaster, solicitor, manager, independent trader, Secretary of State, and the principles or functions for which they stand. The house of Mars imparts austerity, security and generally initiative and honesty ; in weak cases there may be, however, some doubt with regard to his absolute integrity. He may be the authority, who concludes a union, viz. notary, clergyman or civil authority. In the church he is the High Priest, in the lodge the Grand Master.*

Queen

TRADITION : Country woman, honest, economical woman, honourable and loving, virtuous, chaste, good and inclined to be friendly and interest herself in the querent. The card may also indicate love of money, economy and gifts.

THEORY : Queen of *Air* on the *Second house* of economy, money, country life and art. Some of the traditional renderings certify this remarkably well. Now what does a queen in general mean ? In divination a woman simply, but in general, as the king is the head of the hierarchy or suit as the spiritual synthesis and masculine representative, so the queen may be said to be the material synthesis and the chief female representative. So the queen of wands must be, apart from all personality, the representative of banking, exchange, agriculture and of the arts in general, painting, music and dancing in particular. In *W.'s* picture of this card, a cat is seen before the feet of this queen : a remarkable indication of the house in which, as astrology teaches, the moon is exalted. It indicates rightly, that in weak cases there may be some falsehood in the nature of persons indicated by it. Cajolery, but apt to turn into peevishness. Taurus-people are generally good-humoured and good-natured, patient, benefic for their surroundings in material things, but also desirous of luxury and possessions, wealth, riches.

CONCLUSION : *A woman of economical habits, wealthy or desiring wealth, steadily resolved to get at riches, certainly not ' cheap ' ; more or less artistic, may be a painter, dancer or musician ; she is faithful, but may be subject to moods and changes of taste. Honesty may be certified, but not without a certain amount of egotism, e.g. materialism. She is very passive and cool, phlegmatic and not easily to be roused to passion, if ever. This of course makes the impression of ' chaste.' There is, however, a solid sort of sensuality. In strong cases there is real virtue. Banking, agriculture, art, capital, money.* The latter more to be seen as ' money-matters ' than as ' ready money,' and rather papers of value, shares, bonds, banknotes, than coined money.

Page

TRADITION : Stranger, unknown man, young man in search of somebody, extraordinary or at least uncommon man ; postman, envoy, dark young man, faithful lover. Further it denotes an announcement, instruction, advice, tale, lesson, advertisement, something wonderful, unexpected, admirable, unusual. A notion as well as a miracle. News.

THEORY : We have to keep in mind, that the page of *Air* relates to the *Third* and to the *Eleventh house* both. Some of the indications show the mark of aquarian, i.e. uranian parentage, others are purely mercurial. The pages always cover the meaning of houses of Air, as we have seen the page of the airy element—wands—is the most airy of them all. The interpretation is easy enough, and the renderings are quite correct, with the exception of one item : we can never see this page as a ' stranger ' but rather as an acquaintance, a friend, conforming to the connection with the eleventh house. That with the Third house even may bring his personal standing nearer to the querent, viz. as a brother or schoolmate.

CONCLUSION—(From the Third house) : *A brother, schoolmate, messenger, postman or envoy, functionary or official of subordinate position, generally a younger man, sometimes on an errand ; messages, letters, communications, teaching, instruction, lesson, advertisement, advice, announcement. News.* (From the eleventh house) : *A friend, some one in business relation with the querent, or with whom he agrees. Telegraph, telephone and wireless. Intuitive connection, telepathy, invention. Helpful influences in general, helpful people of all sorts, tradesmen, purveyors, etc.*

Knight

TRADITION : Young man, friendly. Departure, absence, flight, emigration, change of residence, desertion, transmigration, transplantation, transmutation, separation, disunion, rupture, discontinuance, brouillerie, discord.

THEORY : The workings of *Air* by a special and mighty agent—for this the knight is in all cases— on the *houses of water*, here the *Fourth* and the

Twelfth, causes turbulence, motion, emotion (though it must be borne in mind, that it *is* not emotion in itself) ; the action of the air on the water causes waves. In the case of the fourth house the knight relates to family matters or household conditions, eventually the father, to internal conditions in society or groups of people. It must further relate to memories and the past in general, because it means the awakening of the sentiments. The traditional conclusions have been drawn evidently in the negative for the greater part, in consideration of the fact that the sentiments generally are misleading. That they give reason for many changes is quite true. In the case of the twelfth house this is much the same. But extending its result over a much larger circle, the mercurial knight may represent expedition and exploration, discovery, scientific or practical, emigration, estrangement, and the ' great work ' of transmigration. It denotes a searching for the unknown, which in weak personal cases may appear as indiscretion or premature revelation, divulgation, profanation, etc. We do not see why this knight should be either young or friendly.

Quite the reverse : On account of the twelfth house there is something inimical about him, and a certain dissension of sentiment may find its cause in the past, in a family feud or something in the nature of a misguiding prejudice, tradition, which will have to be given up, etc.

CONCLUSION—(From the fourth house) : *A representative of the father, or of the family, a relative ; a man visiting the house bringing new and perhaps disturbing influences into it, disturbing domestic happiness ;*

changes in the home, house or family ; memories awak-
ened, divulgation of family secrets or private matters ;
an intruder in the home. A man of doubtful though
not necessarily bad character. (From the twelfth
house) : *An investigator, occultist, explorer, sailor,*
traveller on the high seas, wanderer, a guide through
strange experiences, vagrant Bohemian type, stranger
and sometimes enemy or some one with whom the querent
does not agree and from whom he will be estranged,
however earnest his endeavours to keep friendly,
because he speaks either morally or physically a foreign
tongue. Translation, export, departure, change of
residence, emigration, flight, absence, rupture, etc.
Transmutation. Disturbing influences and people in
general, which need not be bad in itself, and may even
cause a revolution in thought. It brings unrest in any
case.

PENTACLES

Ace

TRADITION : Perfect contentment, felicity, happiness, ecstasy, perfect joy, perfect remedy, fulfilment
of what has been asked in prayer. Reversed : Capital,
riches, opulence, treasure. Something of principal
value or valuable, dear, expensive, rare, highly
esteemed.

THEORY : The element of *Fire,* of the nature of
the Sun and Venus, on the *house of the Sun, the
Fifth :* indeed this card has been well defined by
the traditional renderings, which give it all as very
benefic. How could it be anything else ? The aces
are all more or less a commencement, new prospects,
etc. If you get the ace of pentacles or hearts on one

of your houses in the horoscopic figure, you may be pretty sure that the matters to which the house in question relates will be beneficial and, on account of the fiery element, irresistible. It means the commencement of that what is wished for, desired, and this is what man calls his happiness. It is the spark of the Ego demonstrated in the practice of daily life ; and this is what may well be called the note of good, which also brings good luck to other people. So there is creative energy in this card. Not yet worked out into details, but originally decided and fairly sure to work out in the future in lucky events and prosperous happenings. So there is promise in it and it is above all a card of good augury of a new and prosperous beginning. It is like a bright spark. Even among very bad cards it is the bright spark of hope and good-will, though of course in such cases it may be too weak to conquer adverse circumstances immediately. It may mean further a person or thing of first ranking. A child. A speculation.

CONCLUSION : *Creative energy, fulfilment of hope, wish and desire, good luck, bright prospects, beginning of a new era in life, happiness, good augury ; a child ; a speculation. As to material effects it is benefic without being in itself the indication of riches or gold. It may be a present, a donation. Profit. Promise. Goodness. Favour. It may indicate the person, who is chiefly of interest, and of benefic influence.*

Two

TRADITION : Embarrassment, obstacles, obstruction, emotion, confusion, difficulty, hindrance, unrest, etc. Reversed it is given as message, writing, doctrine, literature, work, book, production, composition, epistle, elements, principles; cheques. Another version gives : " A card of gaiety, recreation and its connections." (*W.*)

THEORY : The *Fire* on the *Sixth house*, the house of Virgo. Now here the so-called reversed meanings in the tradition seem to hold the most current significances of this house. Which once more warns us against attaching too great, if any, importance to the idea of ' reversed ' position. The tradition does not give a very clear conception here, on the whole. The word ' emotion ' is not in its place ; as to embarrassment, this is correct : the influence of the sunny and Venusian fire on this house of infinite possibilities must naturally cause ' embarras du choix,' the difficulty of choice, and the one possibility hindering the other ; giving too much force and attention to little or subordinate things and persons. There can be very little harm, however, in any card of the pentacles suit ; the greatest evil done here might be that too little profit is earned in proportion to the labour given to it. On the other hand this card must necessarily mean good and conscientious work and fidelity of servants, agreeable and satisfactory work, reasonable remuneration, and consequently joy. The agreeable stimulation which it gives to the nervous system must cause gaiety, recreation, etc. Good health is also one of the results.

CONCLUSION : *Good work, reasonable satisfaction, satisfactory results, agreeable occupations, but a warning to use economy in the display of one's forces, means, money and health ; difficulty of choice ; trustworthy*

and *good servants ; good treatment of same ; joy,
gaiety, recreation, etc. Feeling of physical well-being.
It must denote also machinery, technics, abilities in
these.*

Three

TRADITION : Nobility, noblesse, good and generous action, aristocracy, fame, glory, splendour,
etc. Consideration, generous action. The reversed
meanings do not appear at all to respond to a card
of pentacle-nature and, as in many other cases,
simply seem to imply the absence of the better
qualities : weakness, humility, vile and abject action,
etc. Another version gives : " Métier, trade, skilled
labour." (*W.*)

THEORY : The *Fire* on the *Seventh house*, which
rules the contact of the Self and the Not-self, the
relations between both, the executive ability in man.
So this must lead to the idea of well-doing and noble
demeanour, owing to the Sun and Venus again.
Compare horoscopes with the Sun and Venus in
VII. Well-conducted relations denote civilisation,
aristocracy, and the proper expression of one's
relation to the world in his occupation, his métier,
as *W.* has it ; profession, marriage and employment.
So this card has to do with ' workmanship,' which is
well expressed by the drawing of the card in the set
of *W.*

CONCLUSION : *Civilisation, aristocracy, good workmanship, skill, civil treatment and noblesse, agreeable
relation, métier, employment, profession, marriage ;
good done to other people, bounty, profitable relations
in business ; restoration, reparation, beneficial arrangement. A marriage will do much good.*

Four

TRADITION : A present, gratification, gift, inheritance, legacy ; liberality, generosity, offerings, etc. " The surety of possessions, cleaving to that which one has." (*W.*) Reversed it is said to represent : A circle, circuit, and in general that which limits, encircles, holds, walls, encloses. So it may be a convent, monastery. Further obstacles, delay, suspense.

THEORY : The *Fire* of the heart on the house of Scorpio, the *Eighth*, which is the house of secrets, of the money and possessions of other people, of death and sex, of inheritance and debt, loans and delay in all material matters, psychic activity, but much hampering in all physical activities—all this makes clear much of what tradition has handed down. Everything falling in this house is connected with some secret, which cannot be divulged to the outer world, and consequently in relation to this world these things cannot appear in their full light or significance, are more or less handicapped, meet with obstacles and are wrongly judged. It is related to monastic life indeed. On the other hand it is the psychic and sexual expression of the love born in the heart, and it means, on this account, certainly " cleaving to that which one has " in a very personal way. It is the card of desire, attachment, secret longing for possession, which, when not being satisfied, may lead to retreat and retirement. The fire of the heart is here suffering from dissatisfaction or impossibility of realisation. It is probably the least favourable card of the pentacles suit, at least in a material sense. It may hold much good for the future, however. Material benefit in this case will never go without some loss or sadness at the same time, as in the case of inheritance.

CONCLUSION : *Desire, longing, etc., which will be probably satisfied in the future, delay, retreat, retirement, secret possession, legacy, inheritance, loan, mortgage, gift, the former not without some drawback, sadness or loss. Debt, probably going to be paid. Condition of being limited, enclosed, hampered or delayed. Some good which is not within the reach of the querent.*

Five

TRADITION : Lover, mistress, also husband and wife, friend, beloved person. Accord, convenience, well-being, affinity. Reversed they give : Bad conduct, ruin even, confusion, disorder, discord, dissipation, chaos, profligacy. Mr. W. says : " It foretells material trouble above all."

THEORY : The latter saying of Mr. W. is probably correct in any case, but we do not agree that the different renderings " cannot be harmonised." The *Fire* of the heart on the *Ninth house,* that of Sagittarius, explains them all without difficulty. It is the emanation of love, which makes practically the lover and the mistress, e.g. husband and wife, when regularised by civil law, and friends, when between persons of the same sex, sympathy and popularity, enthusiasm, hopefulness, love of travelling, roaming about, which in weaker cases easily leads to Bohemian habits, carelessness, disorder and so on. Society will call this in many cases bad conduct, and find much to criticise. That the expansive nature indicated by this card causes 'material troubles above all,' is evident, because it means that more is given out than received, which in matters of this material world does in fact bring troubles. But of a sort that may be easily forgiven, and helped, if not carried too far.

CONCLUSION : *Emanation, expansion, love-making and the consequences : lover, mistress, husband, wife, friend ; sympathy, popularity, enthusiasm, hopefulness, well-being, affinity. Expenses, material troubles, and in weak cases : disorder, vagrancy, roaming about without aim, waywardness, bad conduct, profligacy, confusion, etc. It is sure to indicate love outside the lines of a legal marriage. Strong individualism, which however is probably ruled by a strong will and a good heart. Brilliancy, but sometimes lack of the sense of responsibility. Travelling or emigration will do much good.*

Six

TRADITION : The present, the actual moment, to-day ; a witness, contemporary, attention, good care, vigilance. Presents, gifts, gratifications, prosperity. Reversed it is said to denote : Cupidity, jealousy, desire, passion, lust and researches.

THEORY : The *Fire* of the heart on the house of Capricorn, *the Tenth,* which is the house of the act, the deed, actuality, position and name, superiors and authorities. Moreover it denotes the actual time in the horoscope. The descriptions given by tradition are consequently correct and to the point. We may add, that here, in this combination, the heart's desire and wish, the impulses to speculate and to create, to make love and to do good, all become active and acute. So this must be a card of practical things, which for the greater part will be of a benefic nature. Good action, which may include the fulfilment of duty as well as giving presents and alms. It means putting the heart into your action, working, acting, doing with much pleasure, conviction and self-confidence. This makes success almost certain. It means good-will and noble intention proved by gracious, charitable or useful action.

CONCLUSION : *Good, useful, charitable action, duty well executed, even where not prescribed by written law or order ; sense of moral duty ; charity, well-doing ; presents, gifts, prosperity, fruitfulness. Things being duly and well paid. Good selling. The seizing of opportunity. There is advantage in acting at once. The present moment, to-day. In weak cases there may be of course some sort of speculating on other people's charity or presents, consequently something like desire, cupidity, etc.*

Seven

TRADITION : Money, riches, sums of money, also silver especially. Has to do with the moon and whiteness. Candour, innocence, purgation, purification. Business, barter. Reversed : Mental worries, suspicion, diligence, fear, mistrust, etc.

THEORY : The *Fire* with its sunny and Venusian character on the *Eleventh house,* the house of friends, in which the Self has to rely for a good deal on them or to live for them, but in which it sometimes finds it hard to give up its own desires and wishes. Still in the main it contains ' friendly ' surroundings and is the house of traffic and business, of practical co-operation and interrelation. Aquarius is the house of the Angels too, and this may account perhaps for such renderings as innocence, purgation, etc., and may mean that the individualistic and egotistic elements have to be modified into something more ' brotherly.' What we have to do with the moon and its metal silver here, is less clear, unless the idea has been induced by the electric-blue colour of this house, or by the fact that it is the first house of the lunar body in the solar system. Neither can we very clearly see why it should indicate riches, money, etc. This is probably a rather coarse transmission of the idea, that friendly relations together with the person's own good intentions and good-will must produce advantages in material things. So the card must indicate good business, profitable friendship, assistance and help of friends and *vice versa*; reliable and agreeable surroundings outside the family circle. The advantages will probably be the outcome of what has been sown before by good action. For ' fear, mistrust,' etc., we can see no reason.

CONCLUSION : *Friendship, concord, friendly relations and sympathetic, reliable and agreeable surroundings outside the family circle ; profitable co-operation, advantage, good business, remuneration. Natural and rational outcome of what has been sown previously.*

Eight

TRADITION : A dark girl, honest girl. Reversed : usury, voided ambitions, vanity, cupidity, avarice. *W*. says : " Work, employment, commission, craftsmanship, skill in craft and business." Another

H

version has also : abundance, hospitality, politeness, kind reception, majority, augmentation, etc.

THEORY : It is the *Fire* on the *Twelfth house*. This has not much to do with useful work directly, nor with employment, but very much with skill and ingenuity, genial finding-out of the nature of things, so ' craftsmanship ' may stand. For the rest, it is the house of offering, devotion, self-undoing, imprisonment and treason. The combination of the fire of the heart with it produces very different effects. Above all it gives skill and bravery, far above the average, outdoing the commonplace, neglecting fashion, sinning against tradition but widening the views and outlook. Dexterity will ensue from it. In matters of the heart it always tends to the unusual, superhuman, exotic, wayward, strange or dreamy. The illustration of the card is to be taken more as a warning against the dangers of this house than as a direct descriptive image of its nature ; as a sort of hint : keep to your work, do not let yourself be led astray or misguided. It is also the house of the sick, the hospital and the addiction of ' hospitality ' may well allude to this fact. Charity comes under it. That ambitions are wrecked in this house is correct in general, still the pentacles are never strong in any evil sense, and they are apt to wreck fortunes or bubble reputations rather than ambitions. With ' avarice ' it has nothing to do whatever, as far as we can see. The ' dark girl ' is another question : apart from the court-cards the *ace* is very often taken to indicate a boy or youth, the *eight* a girl. The cups are generally taken to denote fair people, the pentacles dark people. Apart from this Eteilla makes the cards of wands—*ace* to *ten*—stand for young people, from one to twenty years of age. The reason for this we have not found out. If the eight always indicates a girl (which may be so because the eight always falls upon a house of water, which is entirely feminine in its nature), and the fiery pentacles must relate to dark-haired or even dark-skinned people, then the indication is right, and we shall accept it as far as it goes.

CONCLUSION : *Devotion to what is not a prescribed duty, charity, skill, artistic ability, work done under inspiration, dexterity, uncommon qualities, perhaps geniality or even genius. Researches into the mysteries of Nature ; nursing, work in hospitals or sanatoria, and these institutions themselves. In weak cases misleading appearances, making a useless show of activity. In very strong cases there is an artistic or genial ability, which will be only appreciated later. There will generally be sacrifice accompanying a work. Work for hospitals or prisons. Good card for a medical man or a clergyman. In weak cases there may be Bohemian love ending in degradation, depravation, waste of money, etc., though never by this card alone. On the contrary, it may indicate the conversion of a good-for-nothing to labour. Dark girl.*

Nine.

TRADITION : Effect, realisation, accomplishment ; positive certain fulfilment of what is presaged by the neighbouring cards, succeeding. Reversed it is said to give : Deception, bad faith, vain hope, idle promise, etc.

THEORY: It is the *Fire* on the *ascendant, First house*, and consequently must be very positive in its meaning and effect. The word 'effect' is correct here and everything in the meaning of this card must be positive in its nature. There may be some conceit and self-satisfaction, but not without goodness of heart; self-centredness rather. The person indicated by this card must be a good sportsman and honest above all. So we can see no reason whatever, even in weak cases for addictions such as 'bad faith,' etc. Neither can we see 'prudence' in it, as one version has it. The force in it does not tolerate contradiction nor delay, does not reason, but acts at once.

CONCLUSION: *Honesty, positive attitude, sport, self-centredness and confidence in one's self, self-reliance, certitude, accomplishment, directness, no attention paid to other people's standpoint. Means to the querent : go ahead, you will succeed. Prompt arrival of things. Strong affirmative answer on questions. The effect is certain.*

Ten

TRADITION: The house and the household, economy, gain, riches, family matters, archives. Building —a castle as well as a hut—vessel, ship, race, posterity. Fortune, game. Reversed it is said to give : Fatality, destiny, opportunity, fate, gratification, dowry, pension. Also decision.

THEORY: The element *Fire* on the house of Taurus, *the Second*, confirms again the remarkable correctness of tradition, without giving the astrological key to the significance. Naturally this card must have to do with economy, gain, riches, fortune, etc., while

Taurus, as the vast field of action in the universe, actually procures that which is called 'opportunity.' The influence of Venus and the Sun on the second house is very favourable for art as well as for monetary matters. So this must be a card of a great artistic value, foretelling success in music and painting and an immense love of the beautiful. It indicates possession without drawback or danger, domains, land, estates, but more the 'possession' than the 'house' as such, and probably this has been more or less mixed up in the past, because one saw a possession consisting in a house, a castle, even a ship, etc. These very intricate constructions themselves, however, cannot be under the rule of the vast and monotonously extensive house of Taurus. The card must stand for banking or insurance house, and favour both trades : banking and insurance. It promises prosperity by means of economy, agriculture, perhaps art-dealing. Further every collective possession.

CONCLUSION : *Fortune, riches, favourable chance in monetary matters, economy, agriculture, art, specially music and painting, may give a beautiful voice, advantage in worldly affairs, possessions, specially domains, land, property ; banking, insurance, art-dealing. In weak cases the card may indicate laziness, idleness, dull luxury and the degenerating influence of an existence without trouble or exertion : it is like full midsummer in human life. There may be some fatality in it. You cannot escape this good ripe fruit of karma, nor the fullness of Nature at its height. The attitude of the wise must be : to enjoy.*

King

TRADITION : Dark man, banker, trader, speculator, mathematician, master, professor. Success in mathematics and science in general. Reversed there are given : Vice, weakness, corruption, deformity, etc.

THEORY : Very often the 'reversed' meanings are nothing else but the expression of the lack of the quality given as 'right.' But this scarcely seems worth taking into account, because all qualities, which are not indicated are wanting, and moreover there are cards which decidedly indicate vices, as will be shown.

The King is the higher octave of the ace, and this particular king heads the cross of fixed signs, so has to do with economy, agriculture, art, vast business, devotional service of the church. The general effect of this card must consequently be to afford protection, and as it shows a very favourable attitude on the part of superiors or influential people, though these will be rather young, or at least, not very old. There is above all noblesse in this card, integrity, honesty above all doubt, nor is anything in it which can be turned to evil, were it thrice reversed. The only sort of faults that could be observed in people coming under it would be pride coupled with some vanity, love of pomp, gambling. The Leo-type will naturally dominate the card. Here is a man whom you must go to see and visit, because he will never come to you. He has a widespread influence, which is for the good of everybody who wishes to profit by it, and against which it is hopeless to contend. The card means further everything in the way of sanction, agreement, consent, etc., and gives success in love-affairs and marriage.

CONCLUSION : *Noble, good and honest man ; generally of influential position, central power, honourable intentions, whom you may trust, but whom you cannot counteract successfully ; whom you must go out to meet and whom you must not expect to come and visit you. May be banker, speculator, gambler, commander, general or manager. Benefic influence, wealth, luxury, good cheer. In weak cases vanity, pride. Success in mechanics and machinery.*

Queen

TRADITION : Dark woman, who suggests " the idea of greatness of soul ; she has also the serious cast of intelligence." (*W.*) Opulence, riches, luxury, assurance (insurance ?), security, liberty, frankness. Reversed : Doubt, indecision, uncertainty, timidity, apprehension, vacillation, etc.

THEORY : The higher octave of the *two*, consequently covering the *Sixth house* and demonstrating the features of the noble Virgo-type. So this must be a woman always inclined to help and to serve, to make herself useful, a nurse perhaps, a household woman of good stadding a good hostess. There are also qualities of science in this house, as it is the house of the Academy and Minerva. So she may be as an incarnation of Minerva herself, protecting science and craftsmanship as the Dame of Wands protects the arts. She must have many qualities and above all refinement, though she may suffer more or less from the evil—so far as it can be called—of doubt, and the difficulty of choosing between many possibilities in her nature. She is generous and benefic. Her presence is a good augury and she brings always protection and material wealth or at least well-being, ruling this house of earth. There may be some timidity; there is always honesty, honourable action, correctness and the right attitude to all problems of life, discretion, education, understanding, knowledge. These qualities certainly engender security in life.

CONCLUSION : *A good and intelligent woman, who will render service to the querent, benefic influence, help, assistance in word, advice and action. Woman of good standing and refined type, the personification of honesty, protection, knowledge, understanding, education, culture. Discretion may sometimes lapse into timidity through sensitiveness. Material benefit, earnings, wealth, rent, products. Security, assuredness, insurance, certificate or diploma. Patronage of science and technical and industrial works.*

Page

TRADITION : Dark young man, disciple, student, speculator, commercial man. Application, scholarship, study, reflexion, meditation, occupation, rule, management, news, message and the messenger himself. The reverse meanings are here for once even given as favourable for the greater part: Profession, luxury, sumptuousness, breadth, abundance, magnificence, liberality, generosity, well-doing. Also the crowd, multitude. Degradation, dissipation.

THEORY : The Page, always more or less of a messenger, in this case of fiery nature, on the *Seventh house,* as well as on *the Third.* The latter house is that of the disciple and the message; so here the traditional rendering is again quite correct. The seventh house explains everything that is said about application, occupation, profession, liberality, etc., this being the house of Libra, of relation. We may add, that the card will indicate a proposal of marriage, courting, love-making, but in a gentle, sometimes a poetical or platonic way, not without ardour however. It has also to do with all sorts of honourable offices and denominations and may indicate any official person in the civil service and commerce, a stationer, bookseller or editor, book-keeper or director, appointed by the owner or patron.

CONCLUSION : *Disciple, student, messenger, and the message, good and favourable news; a newsagent; honourable denomination, commission, news about a position or relation, contract or profession. Liberal conduct of people towards the querent. A director, directing manager, bookkeeper, assistant. Editor, book-seller. Honourable mention. Agreeable conditions in general. Application, study, reflexion, arrangement, occupation, well-doing, goodness. May denote a meeting, a committee or a board of directors.*

Knight

TRADITION : Utility, advantage, serviceableness, profit, interest, gain, importance, necessity. Reversed it is said to give : Repose, tranquillity, apathy, inertia, idleness, discouragement ; also recreation, etc.

THEORY : The Fire on the *Eighth* and on the *Fourth house,* personified. The traditional renderings are not bad but far from complete. The eighth house is that of our debts, money of other people and of the dead in particular. So the querent may profit by legacies or inheritance. Consequently the benefic influence on the weak point in our material conditions may be interpreted as : advantage, interest, etc. But the knight is always a personification, too, and this is not given in the traditional interpretation. We must see him as a person who is obliging, carrying out a will, coming to the aid of the querent, secretly or confidentially perhaps, at least not publicly, visiting him in his house, saving him from material and financial troubles. It may be a loan, inheritance or advance, but without any hard conditions connected with it, so it may be a present. On the other hand the houses mentioned give the tendency to retire from the outer world ; this accounts for renderings such as ' inactivity, inertia,' etc. . . . We should say, it means the tendency to enjoy the good things of the heart(s) within one's own private or family circle, in repose, in some retreat, secretly. In weak cases there may be some danger of degeneration into idleness or indolence, etc. In connection with the fourth house, ruling family matters and the past, the home and the storehouse (of memory, e.g.) the card must have to do with pleasant memories, recollections, people we have known before ; collections and collecting.

CONCLUSION : *A good help, discreet aid in financial difficulties, paying of debts ; advantage, interest, etc. And the person who brings these to the querent. Loan, inheritance, advance, present. Happy memories, collections and collecting, recollection ; savings. Persons whom we have known before or who stand in a nearer relation to us than is known or announced publicly. In weak cases : indolence, secret enjoyment, idleness, stagnation, etc.*

CUPS

Ace.

TRADITION : Table, first as the symbol of the bearer of food, alimentation, etc., then also as ' table of the law ' ; catalogue, tabulation ; the Holy Table. Meal, feast, gala, and invitation for the same. Hotel, restaurant, etc. Picture, painting, image, description. Production, fertility, abundance. Stability, fixity, constancy, etc. Reversed : Mutation, change, transmutation, inconstancy, etc. Buying and selling. Metamorphosis, reversal, revolution, translation, interpretation. Another version says : " House of the true heart, joy, contentment . . ." (*W.*) Reversed : " House of the false heart . . ."

THEORY : The Cups, representing the element of *Water,* Jovian and lunar by nature, start their cycle on the *Ninth house,* the house of Sagittarius, ruled by Jupiter, the lawgiver. The element Water has its two polar effects in the soul, so we need not look for particular ' weak cases ' to demonstrate a more or less benefic and malific effect at the same time. The house of Sagittarius, however, does not bring much evil to the soul and is generally uplifting, inviting, pushing towards progress and development, journeying and hospitable reception of strangers. There is little or no stability or fixity in it, but on the contrary always a good deal of ' mutation ' ; also the magic power of the true transmutation. Further we find a tendency to teach, to translate, guide, interpret. It may, too, lead to extravagance as regards dissipation or at least spending. There is sanction or even holiness in it, inspiration, idealism. The latter, of course, may lead to more or less well-directed actions.

CONCLUSION : *Sanction, permission, inspiration, idealism, enthusiasm, blessing. May denote a leader, teacher, guide or any influence of this nature. Legislation, direction, instruction ; hospitality and sympathetic reception. Driving, hunting, travelling ; planning for the future. Invitation, convocation, appeal. Mutation and transmutation. Translation and interpretation.*

Two

TRADITION : Love, passion, inclination, sympathy, attraction, concord, friendship, the inter-relation of the sexes ; Reversed : Lust, cupidity, jealousy, wish, desire, but the card may also give, says *W.,* " that desire which is not in nature, but by which nature is sanctified."

THEORY : The *Water* of the soul on the house of Capricorn, *the Tenth* house of the act, the deed, manifestation. The two souls find each other here in an act, which of course must be that of meeting in the body. Soul-union, ending in bodily attraction. So the traditional rendering appears once more to be fairly correct. It is the outcome of idealism, indicated by the ace, shared by two souls. It is anyhow not the sex-element as a curse, but as a blessing in practical life. The card may further denote any sort of friendly act and sympathetic encounter. We should say, as regards ' love,' it is to be rather defined as love-making, courting.

CONCLUSION : *Love-making, passion, friendship, attraction, concord, good action, hospitable meeting or reception, the interrelation of the sexes, desire. In the weaker aspect : lust, cupidity, ' cupboard ' love.*

Three

TRADITION : Success, happy issue, lucky solution, victory, accomplishment, cure, healing, fulfilment. Matter in plenty, perfection, merriment. Reversed it is said to denote : Expedition of affairs, dispatches, achievements, end, conclusion, etc.

THEORY : The *Water* on the house of friends, *the Eleventh,* must bring concord, etc. Friendship, but on this airy house more platonic than that of the foregoing card. It is the house of surroundings so far mastered by the Ego and on this account ' friendly.' So the soul-life in surroundings that have been mastered will enjoy desirable and ' good ' conditions and feel ' happy.' There is no feeling whatever of being hampered or thwarted, or depressed. All goes well and the general sensation is cheerful. It is the sign of a good time, good luck and general satisfaction. As the eleventh house also rules the blood, it is very favourable for health and eventual recuperation. Moreover this house has to do with commerce and business, and the card favours them beyond a doubt, giving a good understanding of opportunity and of the character and wishes of those with whom we have to do, so that we can supply what they ask.

CONCLUSION : ' *A good time,' favourable opportunities, commercial and intellectual friendship, success, good issue of everything ; good health and eventual recuperation, healing. Being in good relations with people. Light-heartedness, joy, holidays.*

Four

TRADITION : Annoyance, aversion, disgust, affliction, discontent (with his environment), satiety; blended pleasure. Reversed: News, presage, new light on things, novelty, new acquaintances made, etc.

THEORY : The *Water* of the soul on the *Twelfth house*, which rules many changes, and adverse influences and, in general, the surroundings so far as they are not yet mastered, and therefore inimical. Indeed this house brings much affliction in matters of the world ; materially it is anything but successful and in this respect will certainly bring annoyances, but on the other hand new knowledge of Nature's wonders is revealed in this house. Discontent with environment, certainly, but at the same time it shows the querent throwing his future on the waters of new adventure, leaving home and family to wander forth towards new experiences, enlarging the horizon of his views. There may be some ailment of the soul, however, in this house and in very weak cases alienation even. Sentiments not reciprocated, nor understood. A feeling of being outside one's proper environment.

There may be encounters with strangers or foreigners, and discoveries, as results of discontent or dissatisfaction with present conditions. So in relation to these conditions it may mean : failing to understand or to appreciate things as they are, estrangement of the world, which may lead to seclusion; secluded feelings.

CONCLUSION : *Discontent with present conditions or environment; estrangement, unrest, aversion, troubles, disgust; discord, failing to understand people or to make oneself understood. New discoveries, researches in unknown countries or territories, meeting with strangers. Instability, changes, generally for the worse in a material sense, but having some distant aim. At war with current opinions. Better to keep silent than to talk, because one will certainly be misunderstood. There may be " imaginary vexations." (W.) Seclusion; alienation.*

Five

TRADITION : Inheritance, legacy, succession, gift, testament, transmission, tradition; all of them " not corresponding to expectations; with some it is a card of marriage, but not without bitterness or frustration." (W.) Reversed : Family, forefathers, ancestry. Liaison, alliance, affinity, acquaintance, consanguinity. Race. " It is a card of loss." (W.)

THEORY : The *Water* coming on the *First house*, the *ascendant*, and water having to do with the family, we may conclude, that family matters will come naturally to the querent in this case, just as they were swept from him or evaded by him in the preceeding one. Still we cannot see, that the card should denote the members of the family in particular, as mentioned by *P.* and others. Now 'family-matters' may include inheritance as well as marriage, but so many other things may also be included that it is difficult to enumerate them, and none of them is indicated particularly. So we do not think it wise to say anything more definitely about this. The water of the feelings coming on the ascendant indicates sensitiveness and emotion, which may bring sorrow or pleasure, but generally mixed experiences and not without care. There may be material losses in consequence.

CONCLUSION: *Family-matters, care to be taken of them, sorrow or pleasure, emotion, material difficulties ; there may be some advantage and some loss at the same time. News is certain to arrive. Subject to influences from the surroundings and apt to react too quickly thereon.*

Six

TRADITION: The past, memories, looking back. Antiquity, ancient things, etc. Reversed: After- wards, regeneration, resurrection, renovation, etc. Another version says: "Happiness, enjoyment, but coming rather from the past . . ." (W.) Sometimes "new relations, new knowledge, new environ- ment. . . ."

THEORY: The *Water* of the soul on the house of Taurus, *the Second*, house of exaltation of the Moon. The latter is no doubt responsible for the addictions concerning memory and the past. The rest of the traditional descriptions, however, are rather rudimen- tary. There is more to be said of this house: it is full of meaning, as we already have seen, in the line of art, economy, etc. It relates to the country, and in connection with the latter the card will indicate rustic pleasures, enjoyment of country life and restoration to health by residence on the land. Happiness is surely a characteristic of this card, but we should say particularly in a simple and country life. Further we ascribe much artistic value to it, especially in painting, love for the picturesque. It means receptivity for beautiful impressions in general. On the other hand it may denote a love of good cheer and feasting. Good health and good humour are certainly results of this combination. On account of the Taurian qualities it will impart the tendency to collect objects of art and of antiquarian value; also an instinctive understanding of the same, so it promotes dealing in such objects. Appreciation of music in the lighter style, love of the theatre, but love of Nature above all.

CONCLUSION : *Happiness, feeling of riches in oneself, joy, enjoyment, love of Nature and country life; the picturesque, painting, instinctive knowledge of art and antiquarian value; love of the lighter sorts of music and theatre; good health, good cheer, feasting. Receptivity for beauty. The only drawback may be the tendency to dissipation. Taurus, the everlasting, may indeed produce impressions of the past as well as of the future.*

Seven

TRADITION : Thought, soul, spirit, intelligence, idea, memory, imagination, conception, meditation, contemplation, reflexion, deliberation, views, opinion. Reversed : Project, intention, desire, wish, resolution, premeditation. Another version has : " Fairy favours . . . things seen in the glass of contemplation ; some attainment in these degrees but nothing permanent or substantial is suggested." (*W.*)

I

THEORY : If we eliminate 'soul . . . spirit . . . and desire,' words too far apart from the original meaning, we find in tradition a very pure rendering of the effects of the *Water* of the soul on the house of Gemini, *the Third*, the house of the changeful concrete mind and thought in which indeed nothing is permanent, and everything is passing, ephemeral. These effects must be very varied, including the most fantastic plans and conceptions, and 'fancy' is the most fitting word for this card. It will denote many intellectual proceedings and has to do with travelling for short distances, sight-seeing, considering, gathering impressions, etc. The word 'reflexion' is really quite appropriate in its place here, because the card represents the conditions of mind in which the surroundings are simply reflected in the soul. There may come seductive and suggestive images, some of which may be realised, but others will remain just fancy. The description which is given by *W.* is very accurate and points to the fact, that under the third house come nature-spirits and genii, who will eventually help, guide or mislead man.

CONCLUSION : *Thoughts, intelligence, ideas, imagination, plans, suggestions, fancy, fantasy ; reflexions and opinions, deliberations and intentions. Much in this card will not come into physical reality. Short travels, sight-seeing, impressions, views. Changefulness, unstable conditions. Promise and surprise, but always much more promise than fulfilment. ' Fairy favours.'*

Eight

TRADITION : Fair girl, honest, practical girl, honour, modesty, timidity, fear, sweetness, mildness.

Reversed : Happiness, gaiety, great joy, feasting, public rejoicing. Also preparations and dispositions. W. says it means, " Deserting the cups of his felicity."

THEORY : On the *Fourth house* the *Water* of the soul will be in its own element, so to speak, and will consequently rejoice in its existence, swimming in agreeable sensations, the family and the memory, as far as the personal life goes, playing important rôles in the life of the querent. The lunar and Jovian element passing over this house will almost certainly cause the home and family-life to be forsaken or relinquished ; this perhaps may account for the interpretation : " Deserting the cups of his felicity." We should prefer to substitute for " felicity " his family or intimate circle. Changes in home-life, be it for the better or for the worse. There cannot be much of order or rule in this combination, and disorder or chaos is threatened. The strong Cancerian peculiarities, such as shyness, timidity, prudishness, etc., may appear here, but we can see no reason for addictions like ' great joy, feasting,' etc. Feelings, sentiments, wishes have very little chance of becoming reality in this house, and this may be called the true reason for ' leaving the house.' The latter seems to us to be the proper meaning : either leaving the safe and comfortable home, or losing the chance to realise more ambitious projects. Being the eighth card of the suit, it may denote a girl, and cups are said to be related to the fair or ' blonde ' type.

CONCLUSION : *Leaving the house or home ; changes in the family(-circle). Little chance to see one's wishes and ambitions realised. Shyness, timidity ; disorder* and *waywardness. Despondency, despairing of success. Mixed sensations, no strongly preponderant feeling, unless it be that of dissatisfaction. May be fair-haired girl.*

Nine

TRADITION : Victory, success, advantage, gain, triumph, superiority, etc. " The heart's content." (*W.*) Reversed, the card seems even better : Sincerity, truth, loyalty, good faith, frankness, ingenuity, opening the heart, liberty, familiarity, etc. Concord, contentment, physical well-being.

THEORY : Many of the addictions are very suggestive of the influence of the *Water* on the house of the heart, *the Fifth* ; and we can only say, that they are fairly exact and to the point. The card must signify the realisation of hopes and wishes lying in one's own power or destiny, making one enjoy the fulness of life, and adopting the philosophy of Epicurus. There is no evil in it. It shows goodness and a jovial disposition, not only contentment and happiness in one's self, but also, owing to Leo-influence, the love of bestowing hospitality on other people and helping them.

CONCLUSION : *Happiness, contentment, the fulfilment of wishes, bestowing benefits, hospitality, the ' heart's content,' loyalty, liberality, the joy of life, love of children ; concord, well-being ; success, advantage, satisfaction, etc. Joviality..*

P.S.—In the more profane branch of divination this card is called the ' *nine-months-card,*' owing to the belief that it means *pregnancy and expectance of childbirth.* The latter is significant of the fifth house,

the former confirms our idea, that the cups have
to do with months in time.

Ten

TRADITION : The town, native land, living place,
residence ; also citizen(ship). Reversed : Agitation,
irritation, indignation, anger. Another version gives :
"Husband and wife . . ."   " Contentment, repose
of the entire heart " ; and " A person who is taking
care of the querent's interests." (W.)

THEORY : It is the *Water* on the *Sixth house*, where
it meets with Virgo-influences. Now what about
the town or city ? Virgo is " the city which killed
the prophets "—Jerusalem—and the addiction originally will have indicated the physical, sensual embodi-
ment of the soul, in which the spirit is ' buried ' or
' killed ' as the mystic formula has it. This card
may therefore be called, with truth, the indication
of ' the city of God ' which, by analogy, becomes the
physical body, as well as one's residence or native
land. It means the physical and sensatory possession
or ownership. Consequently it has to do with the
agreeable sensation of being ' at home ' and ' at ease,'
having possession of what is wanted. It must also
mean being fully acquainted with one's work. Good
health and wise living. This house rules servants,
food, health.

CONCLUSION : *Well-earned security, wise living,
husbandry, being at ease, feeling safe ; " a person
who is taking care of the querent's interests " may be
correct and actually present, e.g., in the shape of
servants, shopmen, purveyors. The city, birthplace,
physical constitution. (Tabernaculum.) Medicine of*

body and soul. Organic life in the body and in the community, viz. practical social conditions. In weak cases the house of Virgo may cause irritability and agitation, etc.: a weak nervous system must avoid the full sway of emotions.

King

TRADITION : Fair and honest man ; man of business, law or divinity ; responsible, disposed to oblige the querent ; probity, equity, art and science, and those who profess science, art and law. Reversed : Honest or dishonest man equally (⚶) ; thief, brigand, rogue. Vice, corruption, scandal.

THEORY : This king is the chief of the kingdom of the soul, coming on the *Ninth house,* and consequently must indicate the teacher, prophet, man of law and divinity ; the professor, inspirer and great traveller ; sometimes a hunter, a wanderer, or a sailor, a yachtsman. Honesty and probity will be generally his characteristics, but some fantasy may be mixed with it and he may be less particular in details or accuracy. He may be exuberant or even excessive, and this may cause some excitement, but we see nothing of ' scandal, vice,' thievishness or anything of that kind in this card. There is a lively sentiment of justice in it and the person indicated by it will certainly be disposed to render justice to the querent, whether he be connected with the law or not. If the querent is himself a weak or vicious individual, the card may indicate the judge before whom he has to appear. At all events it may represent the idea of judgment of the querent's actions or business. Further there is less of ' science ' in this card than of philosophy, which is quite another department. There is the idea of promoting, inspiring, pushing. There lies promise for the future and likeliness of monetary advances in this Sagittarian card.

CONCLUSION : *Honest man, philosophical or idealistic, doctor or professor, teacher, man of the law, traveller, promoter, inspirer, hunter, wanderer, sailor, etc. The querent's actions, business or wants will be judged and brought to light. There may be some exaggeration, fantasy or want of accuracy, but there is certainly hope and promise for the future. Perhaps travelling on the sea.*

W. rightly observes under this head : " The implicit is that the sign of the Cup naturally refers to water, which appears in all court-cards " (i.e. of this suit.)

Queen

TRADITION : Fair woman, good honest and devoted ; virtuous and one who will do service to the querent ; another version says : " Loving intelligence, and hence the gift of vision ; success, happiness, pleasure, also wisdom, virtue." (*W.*) Reversed : Vice, corruption, scandal, etc. A rich marriage.

THEORY : The personification of the soul on the house of Capricorn, the *Tenth*, manifesting into the world that which it carries. As such this queen is to us the image of the married woman and the mother and of all that which woman can give to man and mankind, by her virtue both of soul and body. So the card must also mean the realisation of hopes and wishes, consequently success, etc. The ' wisdom' is here more of the practical blend, usefulness, knowing how to act with care and prudence. The card may represent a woman, or an impersonal power or authority, whom the querent has to obey, or to whom it will be to his advantage to submit. It expresses a tendency to go out into the world and make a name and position for oneself, and indicates the right moment to do so. It is fairly certain that it will ensure some publicity, renown, fame, or even glory or theatrical success, but of 'scandal' we see no indication whatever in the card itself, though of course 'publicity' connected with very evil influences might end in something like that. In such cases, however, we must not ascribe the effect to the card, which means publicity, but to that of the evil influences. It is a mistake, which we very often meet in the traditional interpretations, to ascribe effects, resulting from certain combinations of influences to one card which is only one of the composing causes.

CONCLUSION : *A good, intelligent, active and practical woman (may be fair), whom the querent will do well to obey and who deserves his full esteem. Type of the married woman and mother. Careful and attentive, of much use to the querent. Loving intelligence ; and practical wisdom. Success, pleasure, happiness, virtue. Natural growth, promotion in the world, position and name, fame or renown.*

Page

TRADITION : Fair young man, studious. Work, application, reflexion, occupation, observation. Profession, employment. News, message ; has to do with business. Reversed : Tendency, inclination, attraction, attachment, friendship, desire, engagement, invitation, seduction. Flattery, praise, cherishing, etc.

THEORY : The Page or servant, messenger, of the cups suit comes on the *Eleventh* and on the *Seventh house*, and has to do with friendship and relations, e.g. marriage. He must be the friend who brings inviting messages, seductive proposals, if not of formal marriage, perhaps of some love-affair or jolly gathering, sportive meeting, or intellectual entertainment, lecture, etc. It is not quite impossible, that the idea of ' seduction ' is connected with it or at least a strong sense of persuasion. If it relates to news, there is emotion in it, news that will affect the feelings in some way or other. Relations will be of a passing nature, but may be very pleasant. The combination of the Water with the Air generally adds much to the instruction, development or education of people So there must be much of all this in the Page of Cups. The effects do not always bear the characteristic of reliability, nor of permanence.

CONCLUSION—(On the eleventh house): *Friendly message, good news, invitation, proposal and the bringer of the same. A young man of a democratic turn of mind, brotherly feelings, international relationship.* (On the seventh house) : *Proposal of marriage or love-affair, intellectual entertainment, lecture, demonstration. Proposal or invitation to a position or employment. Solicitation. The outcome of this card is still uncertain and must be derived from the neighbouring cards. Change of relations and connections, sympathies.*

Tendency to please and to make things and certain persons appear better than they are in reality, either to flatter them or to seduce the querent. It may also be that the querent will be flattered. Praise and persuasion. A man very much open to sex-influences.

Knight

TRADITION : " The higher graces of the imagination " (*W.*). Arrival, approach, advances, proposition, demeanour, invitation, incitement, reception, comparison. Reversed : Trickery, fraud, duplicity, subtlety, swindle, artifice.

THEORY : The *Water* of the soul on the *Twelfth* and on the *Eighth house*. The double influence of water makes the emotions and feelings prominent, relates to the imagination, to deeper experiences and strong reactions of the soul, processes of psychic life, which may end in wonderful success or in less desirable phenomena. It is sure to indicate much relating to the subways of human life and the human soul. This is not always favourable or pleasant, of course, but is in almost every instance intensive, though the cups never go to anything like hatred or crime or real malice. Their weakness is in being unreliable or incalculable with regard to things of the exact world or matter. So in the worst cases this card may indicate everything connected with swindling from sheer mental instability. But it may also be, that the term ' swindler ' (charlatan) is wrongly given to people who are standing apart from the common herd and are more or less occultists. The " higher graces of the imagination." There may be certainly a considerable degree of falsehood expressed by this card : false interpretation, misjudgment, tendencious or fantastic narratives, exaggerated complaints, imaginary wrongs, pathos and what the world calls miscarriage. On account of the eighth house all this may be connected with sex-questions or intimate and private affairs. The card may express indiscretion committed and slanderous reports, secretly promulgated. It has to do with secrets and the divulgation of secrets. But there may be also a higher sway in the emotional realm : devotion, sacrifice, charity.

CONCLUSION—(On account of the twelfth house) : *A stranger, sailor or naval officer, man coming from far away. It makes one forget troubles, perhaps intoxicates. Wine or strong liquors. Merchants of same. Narcotics. Imagination, vision, dreams, poetic turn of mind. Occultism. Devotion, sacrifice, charity.* (On account of the eighth house) : *Strong sexual tendencies, but the power to master them, and extract from them the element of happiness and health : transmutation of inner forces. The latter may also be translated as : changing his aspect of life wholly : going from one state of life into a quite different sort of existence. In some cases : falsehood, venomous reports, slander, blackmail, trickery, fraud, subtlety, swindling, artifice. The evil influences may cause the reasons for the said change of life, which in itself may well prove benefic after all. There is much occultism in this card ; this Knight may be unknown or anonymous but a very important messenger (to the soul ?) At its best he is Saint George, killing the dragon, the Rosicrucian brother.*

SWORDS

Ace

TRADITION : The extreme or excessive, triumph, force. " It is a card of great force, in love as well as in hatred." (*W.*) Vehemence, fury, etc. Limits, extremity, frontier, confinement. Reversed : Conception, pregnancy, childbirth, fructification, production, enlarging, augmentation.

THEORY : This is the first step of the element of *Earth,* coming on the *First house or ascendant.* Of course this has to do with a beginning, a strong outpouring of force, an impulse, and a material one too. Positive activity on the material plane is typically masculine, and this is a very masculine card, perhaps the most of all. There is no negotiation possible with it. It is emphatically ' yes ' or ' no.' One of the primary expressions of the masculine is fructification, and the male action is indicated by this card. For the same reason it means germ, seed. And its natural consequence is conception and childbirth, the ace indicating here also the ascendant. In everything this card means the actual beginning in material execution, which at the same time may cut short something else. It may mean decapitation, or any justiciary execution. It signifies of course a decision, the end of uncertainty or twilight. It is a fresh starting point in matter : ' *alea jacta est.*' And so it may as well mean a strong demand, an appeal. There is courage in it and firm initiative. It may cause pain and affliction, but annihilates doubt, the greatest torture.

CONCLUSION : *Initiative, force, masculine activity,*

seed, germ, commencement in matter, decision, starting point, emphasis ; fructification. Execution, affliction, pain, but annihilation of doubt and uncertainty. Courage, firmness, integrity. May denote great passion or intense enmity. Fury, vehemence.

Two

TRADITION : Friendship, attachment, affection, intimacy, affinity, tenderness, attraction, etc. " Concord in a state of arms." (*W.*) Reversed : Falsity, imposture, lie, duplicity, bad faith, deception, superficiality.

THEORY : The element *Earth* on the *Second house.* By virtue of the Venusian qualities of the Taurushouse, this Saturnian and Martian element, as will easily be understood, leads up to the magnetic affinity of the sexes, consequently to intimacy, attraction, affection, etc. But the idea of ' friendship' is different and not in this card. It denotes also artistic appreciation, founded on the perfect functioning of the senses. Taste for art will be born from this and an exact knowledge of prices and values. It is the card which means quality and essential virtue. Therefore it has been rendered as ' falsehood,' etc., when reversed, i.e. when the innate virtue is wanting. Now in weak cases this card will certainly denote sensuality and lazy luxurious habits, which will be found accompanied in many instances by the desire for money. For the rest we see in such cases the possibility of stupid resistance, dullness, cruelty, relentless opposition and recreation, passive obstruction, perhaps silent, unforgiving hatred. But in another respect it means the will to cultivate the soil, in the literal as well as in the figurative sense.

CONCLUSION : *Latent force, magnetism, the principle of art, artistic appreciation ; quality, virtue ; magnetic attraction, affinity, intimacy, affection, that force which binds by the reduction of the senses ; in weak cases sensuality, laziness, dullness. When badly aspected cruelty, unforgiving hatred, passive obstruction, etc.*

Three

TRADITION : Departure, absence, rupture, delay, division, removal, being-far-away. Also aversion, hatred, disgust, etc. Contrarieties, opposition, unsociable qualities, gruffness, separation, etc. Reversed : Mental worries, troubles and even alienation. Error, mistake, loss. A nun.

THEORY : The element of *Earth* on the *Third house* acts in the way of the mind and mental processes, and must appear as ' troubles,' etc., because it gives the feeling of the mind being burdened, which might easily go as far as oppression. If the burden becomes too heavy, either the body or the soul may suffer severely, and pain, affliction or mental aberration may ensue. This card must generally mean bad news too, the message which brings news of the affliction. It may be a corrective to a too easy and volatile imagination. It will in most cases denote some sickness, as a result of the pressure or oppressed feeling in the mind or in circumstances in general. It may be the result of worrying. The house of Gemini also suggests some suffering on account of distance, separateness, being far from one other. And the oppressed mind, which cannot have its way, may easily denote the spiritual condition of a nun or some one who takes refuge within the precincts of a monastery. In this case, however, the motives are not of the more elevated or exalted order : there is spitefulness, vexation, bitterness on account of unrealised hopes, want of idealism. So this does not indicate the idealistic type of monasticism. The card typifies the worries of the lesser sort of mind, also small talk, evil thought, the wrestling of the inferior mind with matter and all that may be expected from it.

CONCLUSION : *Oppression, worries, being burdened, baffled hopes, troubles, tendency to separateness, rupture and seclusion, pessimism. Removal, absence, delay. Small talk, bitter and evil thought, sickness ; in bad cases alienation. Error of judgment, wrong opinion, hatred, aversion, etc. In general : affliction. Scheming, but not in a good sense.*

Four

TRADITION : Solitude, retreat, hermitage, exile, isolation, inhibited condition, abandonment. Tomb and coffin. Reversed : Economy, good conduct, circumspection, precaution, wise administration, testament, avarice, household, savings, order, etc.

THEORY : The element of *Earth* on the *Fourth house*, house of the home and the sign Cancer. This immediately explains why this card has been said to stand for economy, savings, even avarice and household affairs as well as for many things in connection with the end of life, since the fourth house in the horoscope relates to the end of life, and to the inner side of life as long as this lasts. Tradition is once more very correct in this case. When it enumerates " concord, harmony, etc.," amongst the synonyms of this card, however, there is some discrepancy, because the only thing that can be meant here is ' repose ' or the condition of rest, as that of the grave, in which external differences are lost. So taken in the strictly etymological sense of the words, ' concord,' etc., have nothing to do with it. If in any case this card should relate to business, it certainly does not mean that anything like accord has been or will be reached, but that one of the parties retires or takes his proposals back. It may also relate to the condition of the soul, in which one harvests the results of material life in the world, whether spiritually, by meditation, or materially, by economy. In any case it points to a stillness and heavy condition of the mind. Further, to the tendency of collecting, gathering.

CONCLUSION : *Solitude, repose, retreat, retiring from the world, " hermit's repose " (W.) ; gathering, collecting, taking home one's savings or impressions, meditation, economy, avarice, precaution, testament, and the place occupied at the end of life, hermitage, grave, coffin. The place of the card in the horoscopic scheme indeed suggests the idea of being buried under the earth.*

Five

TRADITION : Loss, dishonour, degradation, defeat, ruin, reversal of fortune, diminution, wronging, bad luck, destruction, etc. Reversed : Much the same, burial, obsequies. It is also said to represent a thief and theft, corruption, seduction, plague, and all that is hideous and horrible.

THEORY : The element of *Earth* with its influence of Mars and Saturn on the *Fifth house*, ruling the heart, cannot be very ' favourable ' in the ordinary sense of the word and is certain to lead to a feeling of being wronged by the world, an inner bitterness and impotence, which hinders enterprise and business ; so these will suffer. And the heart itself, being of precisely the opposite nature, will suffer and find things awkward, horrible, hideous, etc. In the same way this card must indicate affliction of honour, which is ruled by the Sun. Moreover, as " from the heart are the issues of life," the card may indicate vice and a bad use of the inner or spiritual forces. Still there is another possibility, and this is given by Mr. *W.* when he says that this card's image signifies a man who " is master of the field." So he may be if the inner force is great enough to conquer the afflictions which assail him. In other words, it need not be a card of absolute defeat, for there may very well be a good result, but nevertheless it denotes serious difficulty and a critical moment or period in life, in which the querent or some one to whom it relates will be threatened with the above-mentioned sad effects.

CONCLUSION : *Affliction, crisis, morose disposition, bitterness, impotence, lack of self-respect, or self-confidence ; it may be that self-confidence is ascertained by some struggle or conflict ; difficulties, which after all may prove very useful but necessitate much self-discipline. In the same way discipline of children is necessary. Enterprise or expansion is impossible or not advisable. Things indicated by this card may indeed be bad-looking or unpromising. There will be a question of a loss in most cases.*

K

Six

TRADITION : Route, way, path, envoy, journey by water, emigration, manner, expedient. Reversed : Proclamation, declaration, publication, avowal, knowledge, charter, constitution, bill, ordinance, discovery, vision, revelation, apparition. A proposal of love, says another rendering.

THEORY : This is the element of *Earth* on the *Sixth house*, and the Virgo-particulars expressed in 'earth' become the 'ways' that carry the message from the centre, the heart, to the parts of the system. So it is the nervous system and the arterial system in the animal and human body. Thus it must be the way or path leading out into the world from our house or living place. This explains what tradition says about envoy and emigration, though the latter is somewhat far-fetched, and not in every instance will the way lead so far as that, nor the path be trodden until we meet with a ' proposal of love.' But it is true, that the effect of that which this card represents *may* go far and in general signifies the message in the sphere of matter (Mercury is lord of this house), the message materialised. And this explains why tradition says it means ' apparition'—' publication '—' constitution' etc. It is quite correct therein. The message is conveyed by means of the way, path, canalisation, etc., and appears in some effect or other. So it may even be a vision or materialisation from the ' other side.' It may also, however, be the passing over to that side, the crossing of the Styx, which seems to be indicated by the picture of this card. The cusp of the seventh house in the horoscope is 'the end,' in the same way as the ascendant is 'the beginning.' Though tradition has not rendered it so, this card must in many instances have the significance of passing away.

CONCLUSION : *Route, way, canal, conveyance, nervous system, arterial system ; experiment, order of service, practical prescriptions for any service, rules and measures of internal service. It warns that care must be taken for health and the internal service of the body must be cleared, in order to avoid intestine troubles. There may be something of a course, a voyage to be made, a cure or even emigration, if other indications confirm it. If in connection with Venusian influences, sensuality and the expressions of it. If badly aspected : serious illness and probability of the passing away of the patient.*

Seven

TRADITION : Hope, wish, design, will, taste, fantasy. Another version says : " Also quarrelling ; a plan that may fail." (*W.*) Reversed : Good counsel, advice, helpful warning, news, announcement, consultation, observation, reflexion, lesson, instruction, slander, babbling.

THEORY : The element *Earth* on the *Seventh house* indicates the actual and material union of the Self and the Not-self in the organism, as a material building. In this we have to see the ' accomplishment ' or attainment of the Self, that which the Self wishes to join. Since the seventh house represents ' the opponent ' as well, there may be something like quarrelling in this card, attempts to reach agreement with an opponent ; this will be done in a practical, business-like way. A combative spirit, ready for the defensive. Owing to the diplomatic and fox-like qualities of the house of Libra, the querent may, by this card, attempt to steal the weapons of the opponent, as the figure rightly suggests : using the arguments and fighting with the weapons of the enemy.

Tradition is rather elusive in its definitions of this card ; there are some particulars of Libra indicated, curiously enough, but they are not much of the nature of ' swords '—earth. The card must indicate everything in the line of material ability, from the science of the use of tools, crafts and arts up to tricks of abuse. It may equally favour a labourer, an engineer, a dentist, a surgeon and a burglar.

CONCLUSION : *Meeting the opponent, perhaps some fighting, but more probably the strategy than the fighting itself is indicated. Using the weapons of the enemy. Practical ability. Science of the arts and crafts. Tricks. Understanding of practical and material obstacles, and of the work to be done. The enemy will be disarmed, arguments undone. A person of technical ability ; favours technical professions. Success by means of capability, combined with diplomacy. Good care taken. Scheme, design.*

Eight

TRADITION : Critical position, censure, crisis, chagrin, examination, research, control, condemnation, judgment, sickness, calumny. Reversed : Difficulty, obstacle, accident, treachery, fatality, adventure, etc.

THEORY: The element of *Earth* on the *Eighth house*, the house of death and of the greatest difficulties of life, the inner problems and sex. The image drawn on this card may well indicate the blindness of man amidst the dangers of this world and of his own desire-nature. It must indicate physical sex-nature above all. Further, we shall find everything relating to the revenge of matter upon spirit, the latter being bound and blinded by the former, consequently everything in the nature of obstacles and hindrances, pain and affliction. The house of 'avenging justice' may well cause a condemnation, or a sickness which is the result of sinning against nature's laws; patience is required where this card rules and endurance will save the position. In its most general sense it means the binding by the laws of matter, suffering from the lack of money, impotence by debt or material want, poverty. It may be a great strain on the feelings. As the eight of each suit is accepted as indicating some feminine influence to which we are ready to subscribe, there will be danger from an acquisitive girl or uncouth female here, or even sickness through same. As far as material laws are compelling in this world, there must of course be 'fatality' in this card, or at least something from which there will be no physical escape.

CONCLUSION: *Obstacles, conflict, danger, hampering, affliction, criticism, sex-problems of a threatening nature, danger of death sometimes, fatality; revenge, debt, poverty, condemnation, sickness. Patience and endurance will be necessary or helpful. Uncouth female. Incident or accident.*

Nine

TRADITION : A bachelor, priest, clergyman, hermit ; monastic order, monastery, church ; religion or cult ; devotion, rite, ritual, ceremony. Another version says : " Death, failure, miscarriage, delay, deception, disappointment, despair."(*W*.) Reversed : Justified doubt, fear or mistrust, scruple, shame, imprisonment ; timidity, pudor.

THEORY : On the house of Sagittarius, the *Ninth*, the element of *Earth* must of course relate to the earthy side of religion, i.e. the material expressions of it, to the more heavy, earthy, materialistic mind and its ideas about religion, ethics, etc. It is not very flattering for priesthood in general, perhaps, that from this sort of condition have come so many of those who call themselves ecclesiastics, but still it is natural, because the ' ecclesia,' which has been built upon the rock (Petrus = Capricorn,) is served by the teachers or inspirers of it, to be found in the preceding house. In lay language this means : the expression of religion, of ideals and ideas, descending into matter, taking material shape and culminating in the church or monastery, which, however, come under the tenth house, and into dogma and creed under the ninth. Under the latter's influence are the representatives of dogma and creed, viz. priest, officiant, monastic or monk. It is fairly sure, that from the essence of this card arises inquisition and every sort of intolerance, religious intolerance above all, because the materialistic mind thinks itself in possession of the only expression of Truth, and condemns every other. So this card may also indicate all sorts of hard judgment, rigid attitudes of mind, orthodoxy.

For this indeed is the meaning of materialism in religion and ethics. When the material expression of truth and ideals is at its height, it reaches the value of rite and ritual or religious ceremony, which at its best stands in relation to dogmatism as the jewel to simple stones or dry sand.

CONCLUSION : *Dogma, dogmatism, ecclesiastic spirit, scholastic mind, creed, rite, ritual, ceremonial. The persons representing these. Hard judgment, orthodoxy, rigid attitude of mind, ascetism. Intolerance, inquisition. The' fear of God ' may well be turned into hatred of mankind. In weak cases there may be swearing, atheism, agnosticism, shyness, miscarriage, shame, false evidence given, error of judgment. In strong cases the mind is scrupulous, conscientious, and in strict accord with time and fashion.*

Ten

TRADITION : Tears, affliction, plaints, complaints, sadness, desolation, sorrow. Reversed : Advantage, profit, favour. " But none of these are permanent," says *W.—* Power, might, usurpation, authority.

THEORY : The element of *Earth* on the *Tenth house* : Capricorn, of course relates to authority and earthy might or power, and we do not see why this should be only in a ' reversed ' position. With regard to religion this is the mother-church (compare : Capricorn the ' married woman ' or the mother), the materialisation of dogma and creed in a building, a church, chapel, monastery. In the secular line it may be any official building or office and, relating to persons, any official or public authority under the civil law. The card represents material necessity and the limits and corner-stones which it erects. It is ultimately the card of inexorable karmic results, say material karma itself. To the profane this means very often affliction, etc., and the personality may be burdened by the weight of fate. The image of this card seems to suggest this specially. On the other hand tradition is certainly not wrong in stating that it may represent gain and profit, as the card of karma will bring the full measure of material things in general and not only in the way of tragedy. Profit and advantage, however, may also become oppressive and its possibility must be considered here.

CONCLUSION : *Karmic results, whether benefic or malific ; material limits, physical necessity ; authority, official might and power, obedience to the same ; official persons. The mother-church, monastery, etc. Affliction, sadness, etc. In good cases due reward and honest profit, merited position. Possession may become a curse. Fate may lay low the personality. The card is not very benefic for the parents of the querent, or he himself does not much esteem them. It relates to his position in the world.*

P.S.—The cards of the suit of swords, from the ace up to the ten, relate to the respective 'sins' prohibited by the Ten Commandments.

King

TRADITION : A man of the law or robe, councillor, senator, business-man, doctor, etc. " Whatsoever arises out of the idea of judgment and all its concessions, power, authority, command, militant intelligence . . ." (*W.*) Reversed : Bad intentions, evil, perversity, perfidy, cruelty, etc.

THEORY : The King of the suit of *Earth,* coming on the house of Aries, *First house* or ascendant. Whatsoever we may say of the 'reversed' side or weaker cases of this card, a king is a king and always denotes a higher accord, some one or something of principal value and rank. The king of the Martian and Saturnian element naturally is the king of matter and of war, i.e. also he who wins war and conducts the battle of earthy interests. It denotes the dominion and rulership of this element, consequently the military chief. This by the way we are astonished not to find mentioned by tradition, which mentions the man of the law, lawyer, advocate or judge, who rules or guides worldly strife and contention. As the ruler of the ascendant, the card may certainly mean any person heading a cycle of material activity and before all a pioneer on this plane, an independent man living on his own means. While material integrity is implicit, duplicity, doubt, double-dealing or uncertainty are definitely excluded. It indicates material certainty and severity, whether benefic or malific from a personal point of view, healthy or rude, even cruel. But we fail to see what it has to do with perversity, unless the meaning be the over-ruling of everything else, the higher by the material power, and the misuse of the latter. The card means an emphatic Yes.

CONCLUSION : *General, captain, military chief, worldly authority, chief or captain in any branch of activity, man of the law ; power, command, decision, initiative, pioneering, valour, integrity, severity, material certainty ; in weak cases cruelty, misuse of power, tyranny.*

Queen

TRADITION : Widowhood, female sadness, privation, absence, sterility, poverty, vacancy, unemployment, mourning, separation. Reversed : Bad woman,
malice, bigotry, prudishness, hypocrisy, artifice,
deceit.

THEORY : The female rulership of the element of
Earth on the house of Taurus, in which the Moon
is exalted and 'womanhood eternal' is contained.
The house of money, in worldly affairs. So this
card must mean either woman ruling by matter,
material or magnetic attraction, purely physical
charm, or ruled by material elements herself. The
latter may be seen as : ruled by the desire of luxury
and money, or as : overpowered by material difficulties, weighed down under the burden of a material
world. A woman of Saturnian and Martian qualities
is seldom charming unless in a purely physical and
sexual way ; there may be higher virtues, however,
which in this case will be developed by suffering,
such as chastity, severity, continence—from which
it will be easily seen, that sterility, privation and
mourning may derive, personally. Astrologically
the Martian and Saturnian qualities are seldom
found to be very ' benefic ' for women, being very
often signs of an unpleasant character or injured
reputation. On the one hand this card may be a
woman under affliction and severed from her natural
protector or protection—widow, divorced, separated,
though not the unmarried ; on the other hand we have
to see in this card the woman who is paid for her
' love,' and the fact that " woman costs money,"
a fact of more occult significance than the world at

large understands. It is indicated in the commandment of jhvh that ' man ' should till the soil (Taurus) after the loss of the paradisical state. So this card has to do with the material necessity of married life, with peasantry and husbandry and economical exploitation. Well aspected, it may indicate art in general and sometimes wealth after assiduous struggle and toil.

CONCLUSION : *Suffering, afflicted woman, widow, divorced or separated ; or woman of a lower sort of character, hateful, spiteful, paid love, deception in love ; material stress, heavy expenses, burdening ; also exploitation, peasantry, possibility of wealth after enduring toil. In many cases it means sterility, privation. Only strong characters can stand this card. To weak characters it is full of menace and may cause grief, mourning, failure in the face of the hardship of life and unemployment. It may mean the absence of woman where she is wished for or desired. It warns against the evil influence of (a) woman.*

Page

TRADITION : Overseer, artist, learned man, spy, indiscreet person, who will eventually " pry into the querent's secrets." Secret service, vigilance, examination, calculation, speculation. A note, observation, remark. Reversed : " The more evil side of those qualities " (*W.*) ; the unforeseen sudden, surprising ; improvisation. Acting or speaking without due preparation.

THEORY : The Martian and Saturnian element on the *Third house* and on *the Eleventh.* It is very remarkable, that the first series of meanings in this case hint at the third house, while the so-called reversed meanings bear all the characteristics of the Uranian eleventh house: suddenness, surprise, etc. This element on the house of Air, Gemini and Aquarius, must, of course, denote either intellectual facts or concrete results of intelligence. The latter may be called ' proof ' or ' outcome ' or exact knowledge. The knowledge of facts may be the fruit of an elementary school curriculum, of journalism, of spying, etc. But it is justly indicated by tradition, that the Martian and Saturnian Gemini-man is a specialist in unlawful knowledge or in knowledge gathered at the cost of much trouble and effort ; so it may be also knowledge gathered later in life, university extension. Exact intellectual results may appear as : remarks, observations, notes, etc. When put in the negative there may be investigation, examination, etc. All these are truly the effects of Gemini. There are, moreover, the personalities representing the facts. On account of the eleventh house we shall have to note the same sort of results but more or less reciprocal and sudden, whereas Uranus, lord of this house, accelerates the energy of Mars in this element but is apt to destroy the Saturnian vibrations or at least counteract them. It is quite true, therefore, that this card may represent speaking and acting without sufficient preparation and without dogmatic or very formal outlines : improvisation. Tradition was very correct in this. It could not know, that this page, on account of its eleventh house relations, will represent the railway-, tramway- or bus-conductor as well as the constable regulating the traffic, also the warnings of the same.

CONCLUSION : *Results of exact studies, knowledge, note, observation, warning, indication, examination, inspection, investigation ; inspector, constable, police-officer, and their orders ; spy, detective, examiner. Dilettante, one who will surprise by his daring but is not well prepared in speech or acting. The latter in weak cases. Sudden, rather unexpected, surprising events or effects.*

Knight

TRADITION : A military man, officer, master of the sword, master of fencing, warrior. Dispute, war, duel, combat, attack as well as defence ; opposition, destruction, ruin, hatred, etc. Also skill, bravery, capacity. Reversed : Incapacity, imprudence, extravagance, foolishness, impertinence, stupidity, industry, crooked tricks.

THEORY : Finally this element on the *Fourth* and on the *Twelfth houses.* On account of the former we find of course the armed man under the rule of the Emperor, the military man, soldier, etc., but rather the professional, formerly the hired, troops than the militia, which will rather fall under the same house as the police, and be indicated by the page of swords. Another significance of this card is that of painful memories, suffering by ancient wrongs. In fact war is in all cases, be it private or collective, the phenomenon of the outbreak of some ancient wrong or evil—the wrong of oppression on one side or the evil of desire, rapacity, overflowing force, etc., on the other. So the Knight of swords must bear the significance of the bearer of weapons, which avenge wrongs or serve attacks. The fourth house calls the home and the family, the father in particular, and the card may well denote something in the nature of avenging family feuds or the honour of the father or the family. Badly aspected it may mean opposition against the power of the father or the Emperor, revolution, which is quite in the line of the grumbling and malcontent nature of the Cancerian of the lower type. It is, however, to be expected that such opposition will be very much hidden, dark, in the background, not open nor very loyal. On account of its relation with the twelfth house this card may also mean a surgeon and operations performed by him, and, in lower types or weaker cases, fraud and destruction of organisms, whatever these may be. It may further relate here to all sorts of bad passions and to degrees of hatred, incapacity, etc.

CONCLUSION : *Military man, man of arms, one avenging family or other feuds or wrongs ; wrongs avenging themselves ; painful memories, distress in the family, afflictions deriving from past events. A surgeon, operation done by same ; the knife in old sore. In badly aspected cases hatred, destruction, extravagance, spilling, revolt, insurrection, war, combat, fraud, impertinence, imprudence, etc.*

EPILOGUE

E offer the descriptions in this work with the most humble reserve as regards completeness. We are fully aware, that on these lines the last word will not be said in the near future. On the other hand we feel sure, that the key to the mystic system, known as the TARO(T), presented here, does work, for we have used it in practical divination for some time already and it has proved to be true, apart from its theoretical value, which may be judged by those who have studied the ancient mysteries in general and astrology in particular.

We abstain from adding more concerning the practice of divination in the present volume—it will demand another one.

www.ingramcontent.com/pod-product-compliance
Lightning Source LLC
Chambersburg PA
CBHW021334090426
42742CB00008B/607